LOST IRELAND
1860–1960

LOST IRELAND

1860–1960

WILLIAM DERHAM

HYDE PARK
EDITIONS

First published in the UK in 2016 by
Hyde Park Editions Ltd
10 Barley Mow Passage,
Chiswick, London W4 4PH

Written by William Derham
Designed by Plum5 Limited

ISBN 978-0-9930685-8-4

Printed in China

This edition is printed in 2016

CONTENTS

AUTHOR'S NOTE

When I was asked to put this book together my immediate thought was 'what a fantastic opportunity'. Growing up I had always been intrigued by what had disappeared or changed in my locality. On seeing building sites, my immediate reaction was usually 'I wonder what was there before' and then 'I wonder why they knocked it down'.

Probably the first place that popped into my head was Kenure House (pp. 2 & 3). I came across its massive surviving portico first as a child visiting friends, in the housing estate which now surrounds it. When I asked my father he said it had once been a fine big house which had been demolished some years back. It had been allowed to stand neglected until dry rot took it over and it 'had' to be demolished. Previous to that happening it had, he said, been offered for sale by the local council for £1, such was the amount of money that would be needed to make it habitable again. This fired my imagination. Imagine owning such place, for £1, even if only for a day, to be able to wander around it, absorb its details and imagine who might have lived or worked there and what kind of people they might have been.

This, I have since learned, is the attraction that such surviving buildings hold today, and not just for me but for huge hordes of people who visit historic buildings around the country, and indeed, around the world. Only relatively recently have we awoken to the value of such structures, both to our identity and our curiosity. It can be hard sometimes to tell the wood from the trees, to realise that an unremarkable old building you take for granted, that you live in, work in, or just walk past occasionally, is part of the greater fabric of our past, of its people and identity, and indeed, of our *own* identity.

Sadly this awakening has come long after many such buildings have disappeared. It is not the intention that this volume be a comprehensive guide to what has gone, but to provide a snapshot or an overview of a much larger picture of what is no longer with us.

FOREWORD

It is an architectural fact of life that buildings, like people, come and go. They are conceived in the meeting of the minds of clients and architects, gestated through the planning process and birthed on building sites from their foundations up. They live their often very long lives fulfilling the needs of owners and occupiers. And then they die. Sometimes the death of a building is sudden and unexpected, whether through accident or malice. Sometimes it comes through the creeping decay of old age, and sometimes buildings are euthanised, pulled down unceremoniously in their prime to make way for something new.

Lost buildings are not always forgotten. Indeed the holdings of the Irish Architectural Archive are full of remembrances of the departed – architectural drawings, topographical views, models, engravings and, perhaps most evocative of all, photographs. Since the dawn of photography in the mid-nineteenth century, cameras have been capturing the built environment of Ireland and it is hardly surprising that many of the buildings whose images are held on Collodion prints or glass-plate negatives or even in computer memories are no longer standing. In many ways, much more surprising are the numbers that are still with us.

The pages that follow draw on the photographic collections of the Irish Architectural Archive, and other cultural institutions across Ireland and beyond, to present a selection of Ireland's lost buildings (and some which have recovered from what once appeared to be fatal neglect). As with portraits of people, a certain character of each building resonates from the photographs; some we might regard as curious, some we might wish to have known better, some we might even be glad we never met. But this book is much more than an exercise in whimsy or nostalgia. For our built environment impacts directly on us. It shapes us, as individuals, as societies, as nations. Understanding and appreciating that built environment, and the individual buildings from which it is composed, whether they are still with us or not, is essential to understanding who we are and where we have come from. This is why the Irish Architectural Archive exists, and it is why books such as this are so important.

Colum O'Riordan,
Irish Architectural Archive.

Previous page: Tintern Abbey, Ballycullane, Co. Wexford
A daughter house of Tintern Abbey in Wales, Tintern was built some time around 1200 and, following the reformation, was converted into a dwelling and home. It was donated to the state in 1958 and thereafter heavily restored, removing much of its post-reformation additions and modifications, which can be seen here.

Opposite: York Street, Dublin
Shown here long after its large Georgian houses had been subdivided into tenements, each housing several families. Over time a new pattern of living had imposed itself on the houses and the street, seen most obviously here in the painted surround of the shop which had taken over the ground floor of no. 44. Most of the street has since been demolished.

INTRODUCTION

Each age unwinds the thread
Another age has wound... all
Things dying each other's life,
Living each other's death.
W.B. Yeats

To begin with it may be helpful to the reader to describe the scope of what is contained within the following pages. This is by no means a comprehensive tome. Much has already been written on the architecture of Ireland and its various histories – stories both of survival and destruction – and much still remains to be written.

It is hoped, instead, that this will provide a broad introduction to Ireland's lost built heritage, a wide panorama of the kinds of buildings that have not made it into the twenty-first century, and an outline of the various reasons why. It is aimed at those who may know little or nothing of architectural history but who are curious, and for that reason is sketched in 'broad strokes' as opposed to more detailed ones. For those who wish to explore more, a list of sources is listed at the back.

The term 'Lost' has been interpreted with some latitude by the author. By and large most of the buildings illustrated here no longer survive. There are several exceptions however, to a lesser or greater degree. Some survive in one form or another, worse off than they are depicted here – ruined, derelict or, at the time of writing, on the brink of becoming so. Some of the images show streetscapes largely still intact today, but with notable disappearances within them. Some of the images are of ruins themselves, which are included because they are the best photographic depiction of what is no longer there or is fast disappearing.

It is hoped that the images selected will prove, on the whole, interesting and that they may raise some awareness about what *has* survived but which may not continue to do so unless people act to save it.

The photograph

Modern photography is generally said to have been born when Louis Daguerre took the first photograph, as we would understand the term today, in Paris in 1838. In exchange for a pension he allowed the French government the right to present his invention as a gift to the world, which they did on August 19, 1839.

By 1842 a Hungarian 'Professor' Gluckman had established the 'Daguerreotype Portrait Institution' on Sackville (now O'Connell) Street in the city of Dublin. Photography quickly took hold as a fashionable new art form, a business and, for the better off, a hobby. The first photographic society was founded in Ireland in 1854 and remains today the second oldest in the world.

Arguably the most famous photographer of Ireland in that century, and the beginning of the next one, is William Lawrence. In the 1870s he started a photographic studio at his existing toy shop on Upper Sackville Street, Dublin, an indication perhaps of the novelty and curiosity that was associated with photography at the time. When he died in 1932, aged 91, he left behind him a collection of some 40,000 photographic plates, which ten years later were bought by the National Library of Ireland. Such collections are rare survivors. Many glass plates were 'washed' and sold for the price of their glass, particularly during the First World War, the cleaned panes of glass used for glazing things like picture frames and glasshouses. Others were discarded or lost, like the Chancellor and Lafayette collections, when those businesses changed hands. The Lawrence collection is therefore a valuable record of life in Victorian and early twentieth-century Ireland, and many of the images published here come from that source.

Photography of course was not the only means of recording the world in previous centuries. However, for all the wealth of information they can and do provide, drawings, sketches, paintings and the like are always open to that ever-nagging doubt – how accurate are they? When considering them we must ask ourselves what a particular artist was setting out to record. Was the intention to make an image of a scene or a place *exactly* as they found it?

Ogham Stone, Ballyquin, Co. Waterford
Some of the oldest physical structures surviving in Ireland, Ogham stones were markers bearing ancient Celtic inscriptions formed of *dashes and dots. Here one has been commandeered as a gatepost, indicating both the lack of awareness that once existed of our history as well as the resourcefulness that saw so much survive.*

In many cases, yes. But in many cases they chose to present an *impression* of a place. Did they add more trees to suggest a rural ideal? Did they 'fix' or 'correct' a scene to reflect something that was missing or that was, or had been, intended? Quite possibly. Did they frame a scene to avoid including something immediately adjacent so as not to ruin the view and the suggestion that view contained? Again, this is possible. In many cases we will simply never know. Photography was, and is, subject to the same framing and staging, but it is harder to make the camera lie than it is to make the pencil or the paintbrush. Or at least it was back then. It is for these reasons that this book presents a *photographic* record of some of those buildings that are no longer there, but that once made up a large part of this island's built heritage.

The nature of photography in its early days means that certain types of scene are more represented than others. It was more popular (and profitable!) in earlier times to capture the large country houses of the upper classes (and their inhabitants) which littered the countryside than to turn the camera lens directly on the everyday ordinary people, and less so on *their* buildings. As a result many of the following photographs are of the 'Big House' of the locality. However an effort has been made to source images outside of this genre, generally coming in the form of townscapes on market day (with buildings shown in the background) or buildings photographed at a later date when interest in *their* own historical worth began to be appreciated.

What was here?
This leads us neatly to our next point – what exactly was here? And what of it has been lost? In terms of buildings and architecture, Ireland has just as rich and complex a history as anywhere else. The majority of buildings constructed over the centuries could be said to have been domestic in nature, although as we will see these range from the

Thatched Cottage near Sallins, Co. Kildare
Typical of so many vernacular homes, with whitewashed walls,
thatched roof and small, square windows, the traditional 'cottage'
was once a common sight all across the island.

humble and modest to the magnificent and ostentatious. Beyond this buildings were generally constructed to fulfil a community function, be that defence, religion or commerce. The word 'community' here is used to indicate groups of people coming together for one purpose or another, be they an administration, the local churches or the merchant classes. There were various communities, at various times, concerned with various things and membership would have overlapped to a greater or lesser extent depending on the individual.

Without going into Ireland's history too much it will serve to give a broad outline of the country that produced the buildings we are about to describe. Since the arrival of the Norman English in 1169 Ireland was nominally subject to English rule. In reality this only effectively applied to an area of the east coast, centred on Dublin, whose boundaries fluctuated throughout history. It was known as the Pale. Henry VIII's reformation of the 1530s onwards served to divide the country along religious lines, most preferring to retain their Roman Catholicism rather than to embrace the new state-endorsed Anglicanism or Protestantism of the Church of Ireland. Those who clung to Catholicism were discriminated against on those grounds. Those who embraced Anglicanism were rewarded for their support and loyalty. Land was confiscated from Catholics and redistributed to loyal Anglicans in schemes known as 'Plantations' in the 1500s

and early 1600s. When wars were fought (the Confederate Wars of 1641 to 1653, an Irish extension of the English Civil War; the Cromwellian suppression of Ireland from 1649 to 1653, following the English Civil War; the Williamite war between Catholic King James II and his Protestant son-in-law William III from 1688 to 1691) the victors usually paid their armies with grants of land confiscated from the vanquished. Thus a relatively small minority of Anglican Protestants came to hold most of the land, wealth and power in Ireland from the reformation onwards. They became known as the 'Ascendency' as a result of their elevation within society. The Knight of Glin, in *Vanishing Country Houses of Ireland*, quotes John 'Black Jack' Fitzgibbon, 1st Earl of Clare and Lord Chancellor of Ireland, in his speech on the Act of Union in 1800:

'The whole property of this country has been conferred by successive monarchs of England upon an English colony composed of three sets of English adventurers who poured into this country at the termination of three successive rebellions. Confiscation is their common title, and from their first settlement they have been hemmed in on every side by the old inhabitants of Ireland, brooding over their discontents in sullen indignation'.

The Act of Union dissolved the Irish parliament, united it with that of Britain, and created the United Kingdom of Great Britain and Ireland on 1 January 1801. The Ascendency maintained their privileged position well into the beginning of the twentieth century.

With the scene set, so to speak, what follows is an attempt to give a brief overview of the kinds of building that populated the Irish countryside and towns of previous centuries. It is not intended to show a chronological development, as many of these developments happened in tandem with one another, while others are the result of a cross-pollination of different types and ideas. I have divided them for ease into two broad strokes, rural and urban, though examination of what remains and what is published here, as well as further reading, will show that what happened in the countryside was generally a reflection of what was happening in the towns. It is hoped it will serve to show a progression running all the way from the most basic home to the most elaborate house.

The domestic

We begin with the 'vernacular', and at this point it will be helpful to try and define the term. Generally speaking, vernacular buildings were those designed and built without the interference of an architect, or someone who would be considered as such by today's standards. Were we to take this rigidly, it would encompass many of the grand Georgian townhouses of the large towns, largely put together by builder-developers with the aid of pattern books and their own knowledge of what was happening elsewhere. I prefer to think of 'vernacular' as applying to those buildings and structures which were put together by those outside of the building / developing / designing professions altogether. This leaves us with citizens whose skills at building were secondary to their trade, profession or position in life, be they labourers, farmers, merchants or gentleman amateurs.

Near the bottom rung of the architectural ladder would have been that most ubiquitous of institutions, in the imagination at least, the thatched cottage. Structures were and are built for a whole variety of different reasons, but the primary one is shelter – the need for man to protect himself and his goods from the elements, in the first place, and from predators in the second. As such the early ones tended to be quite basic. Walls and a roof would do. To make things as easy as possible materials would be located from as nearby as possible, sometimes directly on site. They would be prepared with as little effort as was needed and put together to form a shelter that would withstand the tumult of the local climate – in Ireland predominantly rain and wind. This simple formula of necessity and local resourcefulness gave birth, via the round buildings within Celtic ring forts and the rectangular Viking longhouse, to what is possibly the most iconic image of Ireland.

These 'cottages' (never called as such by their inhabitants, who would have thought the term demeaning, but rather referred to as a 'house' or 'home') were, and where they survive still are, typically, small structures of rammed clay walls, whitewashed to preserve them from the rain, with a thatched covering affixed to a basic structure of timber forming a roof. A hole in the roof would have superseded the door as a vent for smoke in earlier buildings, and would have been superseded in turn by a purpose-built chimney. They were typically of one storey, long and low in outline. They hugged the landscape in an effort to avoid the elements and were occasionally added to – lengthened – to provide more accommodation. Materials changed depending on what was available locally. Where circumstances allowed or dictated, the typically available materials of dried mud and thatch were replaced with wood, stone, slate and, in some cases, elements of brick. Unlike their predecessors made of wood, which generally didn't survive due to that material's vulnerability to fire or rot, such clay houses survived perfectly as long as they were lived in and cared for. However, the moment they were vacated and the roof disappeared, the Irish rain literally caused the walls to melt and the home itself to disappear. The result is that this most iconic image of Ireland has to a large extent disappeared from many parts of the island where it would once have been ubiquitous.

Of course, there were many meaner forms of abode, of less durable materials and construction (p. 262), but where the typical thatched cottage differed was in its intention to endure, not just for a few days, or for a short lifetime, but for the foreseeable future of its builder and his family.

Permutations of these 'principles' resulted in a huge variety of different structures. The methods and materials described above would have been tailored to the individual and reflected their wealth, or lack thereof, as well as their pretentions. Vernacular houses range from the one-roomed hut or house right up to the 'thatched mansions' of the better-off farmers.

In parallel with these semi-permanent, domestic constructions, which changed little over the centuries, more robust house types developed. Among these were 'fortified houses'. These were a hybrid of the materials and defensive features of the medieval castle or tower house with the form of the more domestic farmhouse we have just described. As with our previous 'type' they start off relatively simple and develop into more studied constructions. At their most basic they were simply a larger traditional house, but the wealth behind their builders, and their need to protect it and to consolidate control of their property (sometimes newly acquired), led to much more solid structures made of stone. Some of the defensive features of earlier castles, like pistol loops, were carried over. Some would have been set within an enclosure surrounded by a stone wall, known as a 'bawn', where livestock could be sheltered. Continuing with generalisations, the thicker the walls and the stouter the construction, the earlier they were built. Other factors to consider are the chimneys and the windows. Large corner chimneystacks tended to indicate an earlier date, chimneys moving to a more aesthetically pleasing central location later on. In deference to structural integrity and strength, windows tended to be placed further from the corners earlier on, later appearing to be grouped together in the centre of the façade. The spacing of the fenestration became more even and aesthetically pleasing later. As well as local stone, brick began to make an appearance, most commonly in chimneystacks. These fortified houses tended to swap their defensive features for more ornamental ones from about the time of the restoration of Charles II, in 1660, onwards – battlements giving way to pediments to put it one way. This came about as the relative peace following the end of the Confederate war and the Cromwellian conquest in 1653 became more established, and the need for such defences less necessary.

The larger of these more permanent types of houses gradually begin to show the influence of ideas from the continent, principally France and Holland in the latter half of the seventeenth century. Following the Confederate wars, Cromwellian & Williamite soldiers and supporters were granted land confiscated from the losing side in lieu of pay. This meant an influx of foreigners, bringing with them new ideas. Their influence is seen in features such as a central projection in the façade, steep pediments, relatively steep roofs, wide eaves supported on brackets, dormer windows and, most markedly, in the decorative use of brick. At this time the idea of a '*piano nobile*', or principal floor, raised up above the ground on a basement, began to develop, and many interiors would have been panelled in wood. Sadly such houses are widely unknown in Ireland today as so many have been lost. An example illustrated here is Eyrecourt, Co. Galway (pp. 242, 248) and one that still survives today is Beaulieu, Co. Meath. These structures could be said to show the first overt influence of the 'Renaissance' on Irish buildings on a large scale. Drifting across Europe since the sack of Constantinople in 1453, Renaissance ideas had trickled into Ireland mostly in the form of small details, manifested by things like carved ornament on an otherwise native form. However, as ideas were communicated primarily through the movement of people, the large influx of new settlers during plantations and following wars hastened the pace of its arrival. This led to the appearance of buildings that reflected more fully Renaissance ideas. No longer was this influence confined to small carved details or elements within a native structure, but they began to manifest themselves in floor plans, elevations and the overall form or composition of new buildings.

The 'Renaissance' is here used to cover any suggestion of a return to the architectural ideas and principles of ancient Greece

Castletown House, Co. Kildare
An Italian palazzo dropped into the Irish countryside, Castletown, with its Palladian principles and refined detail, marked a new phase in Irish taste, culture and architecture.

and Rome known as Classicism. This revival took root during the period known as the Renaissance (through the fourteenth to the seventeenth centuries), when architects interpreted the surviving architecture of ancient Greece and Rome and the writings of the Roman architect Vitruvius, which had been rediscovered in 1414. It slowly made its way across Europe, changing architecture as it went.

The first, and one of the grandest, domestic instances of classical architecture in Ireland was Castletown House, Co. Kildare (sometimes known as Castletown Connolly to differentiate it from other houses known by the same name). Designed by 'the Pope's Architect', Alessandro Galleli, and likely supervised and added to by Sir Edward Lovett Pearce (a nephew of Sir John Vanbrugh, of Blenheim and Castle Howard fame) it is, to all intents and purposes, an Italian Renaissance palazzo dropped into the Kildare countryside, to which were added two wings, each linked to the main house by a curved passage and colonnade. It was an arrangement that would be borrowed and adapted, time and again, to suit all manner of houses all across the island.

These houses are generally described as 'Palladian', deriving as they do from the work of Andre Palladio. He was a Venetian architect who published his interpretation of the architecture of the ancient world in his 'Quattro libri dell'architettura' or 'Four books on architecture' and from these his ideas were readily taken up all across Europe, and beyond. The most visible manifestation of these ideas was the grouping together of the various outbuildings next to the main house, but kept at a suitable distance by 'arms' linking one with the other. To the front these modest buildings were given a similar treatment to the main house so that on approach the collection of different structures appears as one large, impressive whole, giving an impression of wealth and status within a relatively economic budget. Palladio's work was also rigorous. Rules, proportions and an emphasis on symmetry governed the layout of everything – from the size of the rooms to the placement of the windows to the form of the columns and the classical details used in the decoration. From this point of view is it best to think of architecture as a language, and the classical work of Palladio and his followers as being the correct and proper use of that language.

These ideas began to stream into the country, to places like Castletown or the Royal Hospital at Kilmainham in the Dublin of 1680, and then to disseminate, largely from the top down. Buildings, or elements of them, were copied and reproduced by architects and masons from one job to another or by 'vernacular' practitioners who saw something they liked on their travels or in a pattern book and decided to have a go themselves. As the rich imported new ideas the relative prosperity of the country allowed many landowners to alter or replace their earlier tower house, fortified dwelling or simple farmhouse with something more comfortable and fashionable. By this route we get the glorious ubiquity of the typical eighteenth century farmhouse of three to five bays in width, two to three storeys in height, with evenly dispersed, large windows to the front and generally an architectural flourish around the main doorway. In many instances links or arms joined the main house to wings containing offices or farm outbuildings, in the manner of Palladio. Stoic, symmetrical and formal, it was a formula that was to be used well into the nineteenth century.

As with the coming and passing of any fashion, these ideas of classical correctness eventually began to give way. Towards the end of the eighteenth century, and following the Union of Britain and Ireland in 1801, people began to appreciate the idea of the 'picturesque' – of 'cottages', castles and the idiosyncratic assembling of building elements, more suggestive and evocative of the past and of a rural ideal in harmony with nature. Symmetry no longer rigidly held sway. Buildings could be interesting, impressive and pleasing to the eye without being so classically formal. Many classical houses began to be rebuilt and redeveloped at this time to look like castles and medieval manor houses. At first this was a case of adding a few battlements to a building and pointing the arches over the windows. Here we see gothic ornament basically stuck on to classical buildings, arranged formally and symmetrically. With the development of these ideas, however, a concerted effort was made to alter the massing of buildings – adding towers, bay windows and pavilions to deliberately change the 'feel' of them. A good example of such a remodelling was Castle Mary, Co. Cork (p. 193). Many land-owning families opted for a style that suggested a house much older than it actually was, perhaps to consolidate their connection with their land and emphasize their right to it. This may explain the scattering of many Tudor-revival houses built, or grafted onto existing structures, during the nineteenth century. It was perhaps harking back to the plantations that happened during Tudor times, and a consolidation of their right to the property.

Town

The small vernacular homes we mentioned earlier were also among the first buildings to line our streets, when streets as we know them came into existence. Towns were a relatively minor feature in early Ireland. The earliest town-like communities would have grown up around the early Christian monasteries, towns themselves being credited to the Vikings, first recorded off the coast of the island in 795AD. The Vikings established themselves along the coast, at the mouths of many of Ireland's larger waterways. Here they constructed the first proper towns, fortified settlements of houses and streets, adjacent to a harbour. Trade, and the protection of its rewards, was their main goal. With the arrival of the Normans en masse in 1169 the number of towns grew, especially in the more isolated midland areas far removed from the coast. Existing Viking towns were rebuilt and adapted, and many new ones were founded, frequently next to newly-built castles. They were one of the many ways the conquering forces went about exerting their control on the country.

These towns were filled with a mix of structures. The less well off would have bowed to the necessity of local materials and resourcefulness, constructing small huts and cabins of clay and thatch, much like the ones described above, sometimes increased in height, combining a space for working or selling on the ground floor with space for living overhead. The better off would have built structures of thick wooden frames, the walls being in-filled with wattle and daub – this type known as 'cagework' and much like those we associate with Britain today. Sadly none are known to survive. The last wooden cagework building in Dublin city for example, on the corner of Castle Street and Werburgh Street, was pulled down in 1812. By this stage brick and stone were the building materials of choice. The popularity of brick coupled with continental influences gave birth to one of Ireland's largely forgotten building types, the Dutch-gabled, brick townhouse, known locally as the 'Dutch Billy'. Most have long since vanished or have been subsumed into later buildings.

St Finn Barre's Cathedral, Cork

The old medieval Cathedral in Cork, one of the many casualties of 'renovation' in the eighteenth century of earlier medieval structures.

It eventually gave way to the present-day cathedral that bears the same name, in the late 1860s.

Following the reformation, from the 1540s onwards, many of these towns would begin to develop along segregated religious lines, in many instances Catholics inhabiting the suburbs without the town walls, Protestants ensconced within.

With the plantations of the sixteenth and early seventeenth centuries a new type of town made its appearance, especially in Ulster. The new towns were rigorously planned, centred on a diamond or square and fortified. Much as the Normans had created new towns for the same reasons centuries before, these new plantation towns were used as a way of asserting control over newly acquired lands. They formed a protected foothold on newly gained lands, a convenient location from which to administer the new regime and billet a local garrison. Their buildings also tended to be more robust, frequently made of brick. Brick was to become much more prevalent following the restoration of Charles II in 1660 and even more so after the Williamite Wars at the end of the seventeenth century. Following the restoration many exiled supporters of the late Charles I returned home with his newly crowned son, some to Ireland, bringing with them architectural ideas they had garnered from their exiled years in France, Holland and the rest of Europe. A similar influx was to follow at the close of the wars of William III and James II. The Dutch Billy mentioned above was the obvious result of these new influences. As time and fashion progressed these Dutch-style houses gave way to the regular, rectangular elevations of the 'Georgian' town house. Next to the thatched rural cottage, the Georgian street is probably Ireland's most vivid architectural motif – rows of brick houses, each differing slightly from the other, just enough to make the individual house unique but not so much that it disrupts the overall effect of unity.

Community

During the eighteenth century, as towns grew and expanded, many began to reflect the enlightened influences or pretensions of their local landlord. New public buildings like churches and market houses were constructed, sometimes as the focus of newly laid out streets. At this time quite a few new towns were laid out and built from scratch, such as Prosperous, Co. Kildare and Portlaw, Co. Waterford.

As stated, one of the primary reasons for the development of towns was commerce. They were the places where the agricultural bounty produced in their locality was bought and sold. Most were well represented by a market house, usually adjacent to the main square at the centre of the town, where markets would be held at different times throughout the year. These market houses were typically composed of an open ground floor, with arches or an arcade supporting an enclosed first floor overhead, and were sometimes used as a place for courts to meet or for other administrative purposes. Many survive, albeit most now with their ground floor arcade filled in to create accommodation for some new purpose. Several have been completely lost, notably that at Mountrath, Co. Laois (p. 90).

In addition to a market house, commerce was architecturally visible in towns in the form of shops. In the earliest instances a shop was simply a room in a house. Little indication of this was given – perhaps a sign over the door, or in the window. Later the presence of a shop would become more obvious. Gradually the shop window became more pronounced and a second, separate door was added. Eventually an individual shop 'front' emerged and the majority of the ground floor was given over to commerce. Windows were enlarged, more prominent signage appeared. However, in most cases, especially where the building was not constructed with the purpose of a shop in mind, the shop front remained framed within the façade of the house. The 'front' would remain one element within the overall façade of the building. Typically it would be composed of a door next to a large window, or set between two such windows. Later, the shop front came to take up all, or almost all, of the ground floor, with the entrance to the home over the shop being a discreet door within the overall shop front composition, or relegated to one side of it. As a merchant middle class emerged and grew more prosperous, so these shop fronts became more and more elaborate.

If commerce was the main reason people came together in settlements, once they had done so their other needs had to be tended to, and principal among these was religion. Following the reformation, from 1536, Anglicanism became the official religion of the state, and other faiths were suppressed, to a greater or lesser extent, over the following centuries. Medieval churches and cathedrals were appropriated to Anglicanism as the newly established religion of the state, where previously they would have been Roman Catholic. Many new Anglican churches were built, old structures renovated or replaced, and a huge amount of money and artistry expended in consolidating and promoting the position of this new Church of Ireland. A good example of this is St Finn Barre's Cathedral in Cork City. The old medieval cathedral was replaced, with the exception of its steeple, with a new classically designed church in 1735 (opposite, also p. 185), which in turn gave way to that which we can see today. In parallel with this aggrandisement of the Church of Ireland, the places of worship of other faiths (mostly Roman Catholic as well as Presbyterian and Methodist) were reduced to being modest, sometimes even hidden structures. Catholic churches, for instance, were forbidden at one time to have a steeple or bells. This resulted in a type of vernacular building generally having a rectangular plan, much like a barn. Sometimes small transepts were added, turning the plan into a 'T'. Many of these also functioned as schools and were occasionally used for threshing corn. Large windows, and occasionally some decorative flourishes, indicated the building's purpose was more than agricultural. In the decades following Catholic emancipation in 1829, new Catholic churches sprang up in almost every town and village across the island. Many replaced the earlier mass-houses just described. The result was the unfortunate loss of a whole swathe of vernacular buildings across the country. In the case of St Mary's in Clonmel, Co. Tipperary, the new church was built around the old one, which was then demolished in the space of six days and its rubble hidden beneath the new floor. Parishioners went to mass in the old church one Sunday and the new church the following weekend.

The administration and security of towns gave rise to a whole infrastructure of other buildings, including barracks, courthouses, prisons, workhouses, schools and banks. Many new barracks were constructed at the end of the eighteenth and start of the nineteenth centuries in response to the threat from Napoleonic France. Most followed the example set by the Royal Barracks (now Collins' Barracks) begun in Dublin in 1704 – large multi-storied ranges of dormitories and rooms set above stables and communal spaces. Typically they would be arranged around several sides of a large open parade ground and have as their architectural focus a cupola and clock over an arched entrance. Many more barracks of a much more modest and unassuming, even domestic, nature were constructed for the Irish Constabulary (from 1867 the Royal Irish Constabulary or RIC) following its creation in 1822.

Courts and gaols, previously housed in parts of other structures like the market house mentioned above or in old defensive buildings like castles, began to get new buildings of their own. The early part of the nineteenth century saw a reordering of the legal system in Ireland and with that new courthouses, gaols and penitentiaries mushroomed up in towns across the island. These were generally sombre constructions, wearing their seriousness on their sleeves, so to speak. Some, however, were thoroughly impressive, perhaps reflecting the pretensions of the Grand Juries who would have administered justice and local government from within them.

1836 saw the passing of the Poor Law Act, under which the island was divided up into 130 Poor Law 'Unions', each with the responsibility to build and run a workhouse. The workhouse, a word that still sends shivers down Irish spines, was a place of last resort, where the destitute threw themselves on the charity of the state. Whole families did so and were immediately split up, women

in one wing, men in another; the sexes then subdivided by age; boys and girls separated from father and mother. They were modelled on the similar system in England but gained added notoriety on this island during the Great Famine of 1845–52. During that awful time they were woefully oversubscribed, degenerating into hell-like places of Dickensian imagination. Each was surrounded by a large wall, making those who entered *de facto* prisoners of its system of 'charity'. Large numbers later became hospitals or infirmaries, and many were demolished to make way for hospitals in the early twentieth century. A similar building of righteous Victorian do-goodery was the asylum, many being constructed in the 1840s.

On the more progressive side of things the nineteenth century also saw the rolling out of institutions such as the bank, the school and the public water fountain. From 1831 National schools began to appear under the auspices of the National Board of Education. They were typically formed of two large schoolrooms, divided by sex, with separate entrances for each. Banking began to grow, with the Provincial Bank being established in 1825, the National Bank being set up by Daniel O'Connell in 1835 and many regional banks, like the Ulster Bank, the Royal Bank and the Munster Bank following suit. By 1878 there were 403 branches of various banks spread out across the towns of Ireland. They are generally imposing stone structures with a well-lit banking hall housed on the ground floor and offices above.

The great totem of the reign of Queen Victoria was of course the Industrial Revolution. With the exception of the north-east of the island, in Ulster, it never reached the heights seen in Britain. The infrastructure of industrialisation – mills, distilleries, and workshops – did make an appearance on most parts of the island, but never to the extent, or on the scale, that they did across the Irish sea. One particular exception was the railways. Ireland's first railway linked the port town of Kingstown, Co. Dublin (now Dun Laoghaire), an important stop on the journey to and from England, to the city of Dublin in 1834. Within a very short space of time many companies followed suit, linking different parts of the island via rail. The infrastructure associated with the railways included stations, signal boxes, sheds and yards. Individual railway companies also established hotels near their larger stations to capitalise on the potential for holidays and leisure travel of the newly emerging middle classes – another creation of the nineteenth century. Railways continued to expand, disparately, reaching their peak in the 1920s with over 5,600 km (3,500 miles) of track laid across the island.

The end of an Era

By no means all of the building types described above have disappeared, but change is inevitable. It is happening all the time and the appearance of many of Ireland's greatest surviving buildings today is the result of centuries of history having been acted upon them – they have been altered or added to, attacked or defended, neglected or restored. Others, however, have completely succumbed to it. What follows will give some brief historical context for later events.

Despite the progress of the nineteenth century, particularly in terms of infrastructure, it is often said, with some justification, that the reign of Queen Victoria was an unhappy time for Ireland. As well as encompassing the Great Famine, which still lives vividly in the Irish memory and imagination, it also saw the rise of the working people, the birth of the middle class and the challenging of ideas and institutions whose position had been taken for granted for centuries. In Ireland those institutions that came under most continuous assault were the country's subjugation to Britain and the ownership of land.

From the 1850s tenant farmers on the large estates, many of which had been amassed during plantations or following wars, began to demand better treatment at the hands of their landlords. Fair rents and fixity of tenure were high on their list of demands. Agitation for better treatment, through a representative association known as the Land League, would eventually break out into a 'Land War'. The question of land was one of the dominating features of the latter part of nineteenth century Ireland. In response several Acts of Parliament, known as the Land Acts, were introduced, beginning in 1870, which granted rights to tenants, fixing fair rents and allowing them to purchase their holding from their landlord. A Land Commission was created in 1881 under the second Land Act to establish fair rents. With the Ashbourne Act of 1885 the Commission's main task became the redistribution of land among Irish tenant farmers, who were subsidized in buying their holdings through government loans. One of the most significant of these Acts was the Wyndham Land Purchase Act of 1903, which offered landlords a 12% bonus to sell. The incentive encouraged many to sell off their large estates, keeping only the land immediately surrounding their house, known as a demesne. Although benefitting tenants, when landlords disposed of their whole estates it deprived them of their primary source of income and would later impact on their ability to maintain their homes. By 1920 the Land Commission had supervised the transfer of 13.5 million acres from landlord to tenant across the island.

The struggle over land played out in tandem with the demand of many in Ireland for a devolved parliament to govern Irish affairs, as had been the case up until 1801. Such a measure was known as 'Home Rule'. Although supported by a large majority of the population, a sizeable minority, mostly Protestant and based in the north-east of the country, were resolutely opposed to the idea. They were known as Unionists for their support of the union between

The Four Courts, Dublin
Shown here following the heavy shelling it suffered in 1922, during *which it lost its dome. It was one of the great losses of the Civil War, though thankfully it was rebuilt afterward.*

Great Britain and Ireland and feared that their concerns and interests would be ignored, or even abused, by a Home Rule parliament that would be composed mostly of Catholic Nationalists.

In the latter part of the nineteenth century the Irish Parliamentary Party, led by Charles Stewart Parnell and, from 1900, by John Redmond, were in the happy position of holding the balance of power between the two main political parties in Britain, the Liberals and the Conservatives. Through this position of influence three Home Rule bills were introduced into Parliament in Westminster in 1886, 1895 and 1912. The last of these passed but due to legislative procedure was not due to come into effect until 1914.

With the passing of the Home Rule Act in 1912, both sides of the political divide in Ireland began to consolidate their position. In Ulster local Unionist militias had been formed as early as 1911 and were brought together in 1913, forming the Ulster Volunteer Force (UVF). Their aim was to resist any attempt to impose Home Rule on Ulster. In reaction to this, in the same year, Nationalists founded the Irish Volunteers, with the aim of securing for Ireland what had already been decided by Parliament. Both volunteer forces acquired arms to equip their men and set about drilling and practicing manoeuvres. In effect two well-armed, private armies now stood facing each other, waiting for the government in Westminster to make the next move. The 'Curragh Mutiny' threw the situation into even starker relief. As tensions mounted the government ordered army troops into Ulster to guard ammunition depots. Fearing that they were being manoeuvred into a position where they would be ordered to fight the UVF, whose aims many would have supported, forty-eight officers offered their resignations. The government moved to clarify the orders and in the process the Secretary of State for War made a promise that the army would not be used against Ulster Unionists in a Home Rule war. A more combustible and unresolvable situation is hard to imagine.

The Decade of Change

The outbreak of the First World War in July 1914 came at a convenient time for the political crises in Ireland. A stay was put on all plans, each side allowing itself to believe that participation in the ranks of the British forces (conscription wasn't introduced in Ireland) would see their loyalty rewarded with a better solution than that on offer at the end of 1914. Indeed, with the enlisting of thousands of men from either side of the political divide, it was hoped by some that fighting together side by side might cause them to see beyond the purely political realm and come to an agreement on more friendly, comradely terms than would have been thought possible before the war.

Such naive hopes were rudely dashed on Easter Monday of 1916. The chaotic rebellion that erupted, concentrated in Dublin, was initially thought extremist, not just by the British administration in Dublin Castle but also by the population at large. However, the martyrdom of the leaders of the rising, and the linking of the revolt with the new political party of Sinn Féin, caused a complete change in the political tone of the country. Most Irish people were no longer content to wait for the changes proposed before the war. They now came around to the point of view of the rebels and aspired to complete separation between Ireland and Britain.

The Easter Rising brought wholesale destruction to a large part of the centre of Dublin. A huge expanse of O'Connell Street (pp. 1, 51) and its surrounds was laid waste, notably the General Post Office, which the rebels had made their headquarters. Many other buildings, which had been occupied during the rebellion, sustained heavy damage, but not to the extent that Dublin's main boulevard did. It is fair to say that it has never really recovered. The damage caused in this area by the Rising was later compounded by the Civil War, which saw a large part of what had survived the rebellion go up in flames.

Following the Rising and the end of the First World War elections were held in 1918. The vast majority of those returned as MPs for Ireland (73 out of 105) decided to make good on the 1912 Home Rule proposals and the spirit of 1916. Instead of taking up their seats in Westminster they formed a separate parliament for Ireland, Dáil Éireann. This met in Dublin's Mansion House on January 21, 1919 and declared Ireland a republic. On the same day two members of the RIC were shot dead in Tipperary. This is taken by many as the starting point of the War of Independence. It was fought between the forces of the British administration and those of the newly declared republic, the Irish Republican Army (not to be confused with the IRA of 1969 onwards). It lasted until the end of 1922 and was followed immediately by a bitter civil war that dragged on until 1923.

The War of Independence was a guerrilla war that erupted just less than three years after the Rising. Its main casualties, architecturally speaking, were to be a large portion of the 'big houses' dotted across the island. In its early stages its efforts were concentrated on raiding RIC barracks and country houses for arms, with these weapons then used against their original owners. The aim, and eventual result, was to reduce the effective control of the RIC, and a large portion of the island was left without the protection of the established forces of the law. Their more isolated barracks were attacked and then destroyed to prevent them being reoccupied. Terence Dooley, in *The Decline of the Big House in Ireland*, relates

Castle Bernard, Co. Cork

Inspecting the interior of Castle Bernard following its destruction by fire in 1921, during the Civil War. Many similar 'big houses' suffered the same fate.

that in the first three months of 1920 approximately 500 RIC barracks and huts were abandoned, 424 of which were destroyed by the IRA to prevent their reoccupation. With the loss of so many outposts from which to enforce, or try to enforce, law and order, attention turned to the large country houses, many of whose owners had left in favour of seeing out the revolutionary period in Britain. These vacant, substantial and robust structures became an inviting prospect, to both sides.

Rumours, founded on information intercepted from the British authorities, began to circulate that many were to be taken over to rehouse homeless RIC forces. Pre-emptively, local IRA battalions acted to stop this, the most effective way of doing so being to burn them, rendering them useless. The first such sacrifice, on 4 February 1920, was Summerhill, Co. Meath (pp. 116, 125). It marked the beginning of a distinct military strategy on behalf of the IRA, but one that was brought about by necessity more than spite. In total, Dooley estimates that 76 houses were burnt between the opening of the war in 1919 and the calling of a truce between the admin-

istration's forces and the IRA on 11 July 1921. Of that, 33 were destroyed in the last two months, as fighting intensified.

It was not just the 'big house' that suffered. In 1920 the British government began reinforcing the ailing ranks of the RIC with a reserve force, the first of whom arrived in March of that year. This force was mainly drawn from the ranks of ex-soldiers, recently returned from the First World War, and quickly gained a reputation for violence and brutality. They became known as the 'Black and Tans' as a result of their improvised uniforms of British army khaki and RIC dark green or 'black'. These were supplemented by a force of 'temporary cadets' drawn from ex-army officers, which became known as the 'Auxiliaries'. The 'Tans', as both forces were often referred to, became noted for carrying out arbitrary reprisals, sanctioned by government, on the local civilian population, generally in response to IRA attacks on the administration forces. Many ordinary innocent civilians died, and many more found their houses burned as a result of suspected association with the IRA. This only increased the sympathy local populations had for the IRA. As fighting intensified whole towns were sacked and set alight by the Auxiliaries and the Black and Tans, including Balbriggan, Co. Dublin; Tralee, Co. Kerry and, famously, a large part of the city centre of Cork, which was burnt in December 1920. Here the British forces went as far as cutting the hoses of those fighting the fire to prevent them tackling the flames. Of Cork's notable losses during its burning, the City Hall (p. 189) is particularly missed. Later Dublin was to suffer a similar loss. In a decision to move away from guerrilla fighting and to create a public show of force, the IRA captured and set fire to the Custom House in May 1921. It burned for five days, taking with it not just one of Dublin's finest buildings, but hundreds of years' worth of local government records.

The escalation of violence, with little tangible gain, convinced both sides that a stalemate had been reached and a truce was eventually called. Talks were held, which culminated in the signing of the Anglo-Irish Treaty in December. The treaty provided for the partitioning of the island. Six counties in the north-east, with largely Protestant populations, were given the chance to opt out of the settlement and remain part of the United Kingdom, which they did, becoming 'Northern Ireland'. The remaining twenty-six counties became the 'Irish Free State' (and from 1949, the Irish Republic), a self-governing dominion within the British Commonwealth, but not a republic. Its legislators also had to swear an oath of allegiance to the King, who was recognised as the official head of state. The terms of the treaty were passionately debated by the Dáil, and eventually passed by the narrow margin of 64 votes to 57. Such a split was immediately replicated in the forces of the IRA. Those who opposed the treaty were known as 'irregular' troops, those who supported it as 'regular' or 'free state' forces. As the British forces pulled out of Ireland in the summer of 1922, they handed over their barracks, stations and arms to the IRA as it was beginning to fracture along the lines of the treaty. This left the country, and its military assets, divided between the two, effectively arming each against the other.

In April the irregulars captured the Four Courts building in Dublin. In the hope of reaching a compromise they were left there until June, but the integrity of the new Free State meant the building had to be taken and the threat removed. It was heavily shelled by the regular forces, with guns borrowed from the British, and almost completely destroyed. The Four Courts complex, as well as containing a magnificent Law Library (pp. 17, 57) also housed the Public Record Office. Dispute still remains as to the intention, but during the fighting several bombs, which had been either stored or planted within it, as well as a large amount of gelignite, exploded. The building was gutted and the written records of Ireland, which stretched back to medieval times, incinerated. Forced to evacuate the Four Courts, the irregular troops continued their fighting in the streets, notably the network of streets around O'Connell Street, destroying much of what was left of Dublin's finest street after the 1916 rising. Victory eventually went to the forces of the new Free State after a week of fierce fighting.

With Dublin retaken, fighting next spread to the rest of the country, especially Munster, where support for the anti-treaty forces was strongest. Devoid of many barracks, which had been occupied by the Free State or destroyed during the War of Independence, attention again turned to the large country houses. Perhaps aware of their own diminishing position, and intent on making a show of force from soft targets, the irregular forces chose to burn a huge number of these, both occupied and vacant. During the eleven months of the civil war Dooley estimates that 199 were lost to flame. Families, or their servants who had been left as caretakers, were woken up and ordered to leave. Most lived in fear of the ominous knock at the door about 8pm or 9pm that usually announced the coming devastation. Ignoring it led to the door being smashed in. In most cases the inhabitants would be given a few minutes to gather up their personal belongings, but generally not the furniture, paintings or silver that furnished many of these mansions. The arsonists would then go through the rooms, piling the furniture up in the middle of each and sprinkling it with petrol. The windows would be broken to help fan the flames. Hay or straw, also sprinkled with petrol, was sometimes scattered about to help start things off. In the most extreme cases homemade bombs were added to the cocktail to ensure complete destruction. Where

The International Bar, Belfast
Situated on the corner of York Street and Donegall Street, this image gives some idea of what was lost during the blitz in May of 1941.

contents were lucky enough to be saved they were soon after looted, frequently from the front lawn. Despite this, few of the occupants came to any harm, with some going as far as to remark on the politeness of the attackers. It was an attack on architecture and what it was perceived to represent.

It is odd at first glance that the big house was to find itself in greater danger during the civil war than it had been during the War of Independence. As totemic symbols of all that was considered 'British' it could have been expected that they would have been much more obvious targets in a war against Britain. Many of their occupants were involved with or associated with the machinery of the British administration in Ireland at the time. Many were also Protestant. Despite this most of the burnings that took place during the War of Independence seem to have been largely motivated by

odds with the perception, it was the perception that mattered and these buildings offered themselves as obvious and easy targets when the notion of revenge or reprisal, possibly born of frustration at losing the fight against the Free State, came to mind. Such burnings were widely criticised in the press. Many owners, although landlords, had been considered good ones. Some were even inclined towards Irish independence themselves. The cost of compensating them for their loss was a particular worry, given that the money would have to be raised through an increase in local rates. Where would the money come from in a war-ravaged infant state with many more pressing concerns?

The answer was that it simply didn't. Initially local authorities were responsible for paying compensation for property damaged in their jurisdictions up until the truce of July 1921. An application was made to the county court and the judge decided whether it was to be paid or not. Such compensation was to be met by an increase in local rates. It was obvious as the fighting wore on that local authorities would not be able to meet such economic demands. The issue of compensation was passed from the local authorities to the state under the terms of the Anglo-Irish treaty. This established the Shaw Commission to review claims and make awards. They reviewed claims made prior to the Anglo-Irish Treaty, and as there was little or no money available, simply reduced them. Responsibility for damage caused after the truce of 1921 was passed back to the local authorities. Again claims for compensation were drastically reduced due to lack of funds. In many cases terms were attached to encourage people not to claim the full amount awarded them. A larger (but still insufficient) sum was offered to many on condition that an existing burnt-out house was rebuilt, or a lesser sum if a smaller house was built to replace that lost. An even smaller sum was awarded if the owner decided not to rebuild. Understandably many chose not to claim their full award. The sum offered wouldn't have come close to covering construction costs. One of the examples Dooley gives is that of Summerhill, Co. Meath. A claim was made in September 1921 amounting to £100,000 for the house and £30,000 for its contents. The judge awarded £65,000 for the house and £11,000 for the contents. When this was reviewed in 1922 the award for the house was reduced to £16,755, £12,000 of which was conditional on rebuilding the old mansion or building a new house. On appeal this was increased to £27,500 for the house, with no rebuilding conditions, and £16,500 was added to cover the contents. Out of a total claim for £130,000 the final award was £44,000. In light of such stringency it isn't surprising that many houses remained burnt-out ruins, littering to this day the countryside they once ornamented.

strategic military considerations, however dubious they may have been in some instances. During the civil war these houses again became targets, this time for a variety of reasons, both because of who occupied them and fear of their being used by the Free State forces as temporary garrisons. The breakdown and subsequent lack of law and order in the period also helped make them more inviting targets. The Free State government had appointed a number of Unionists to its senate in an effort at conciliation and allaying Unionist fears of an independent Ireland. Their homes were considered justifiable targets by the irregular forces. So too were those of former Irish Unionist Party members or those who had served in the British army. It could be argued that as the irregular position became less and less viable, desperation allowed many personal and traditional grievances to be revenged under the cloak of the anti-treaty cause. Despite the redistribution of land under the Land Acts, the perception remained that the owners of these rural mansions were the 'occupiers' of land, taken from the native Irish during the plantations and wars of the preceding centuries. While in some cases the reality was distinctly at

The new States

The government of the new Free State, perhaps surprisingly given the revolutionary flames from which it had been born, treated its architectural inheritance with a certain amount of benign respect. Whether this was down to financial constraint or actual appreciation of Ireland's architectural history is open to debate. Both factors likely played a role to a greater or lesser extent. When it came to housing the new Irish parliament consideration was given to some unlikely structures. Thought was given to rebuilding the Four Courts to house the new assemblies. Plans, now in the National Archives of Ireland, were drawn up for a possible conversion of the Royal Hospital at Kilmainham in which the Dáil would occupy the great hall and the Senate the chapel. In the interim the Minister for Finance, Michael Collins, had established the Dáil in the lecture theatre of the Royal Dublin Society at Leinster House, the largest and one of the grandest of Dublin's Georgian mansions. The Senate was accommodated in part of the adjoining National Museum. In the end this location proved adequate. The building was purchased from the RDS in 1924 and subsequently fitted out for more long-term occupation.

Following the deaths of Michael Collins, assassinated in August 1922, and of Arthur Griffith, President of the Dáil, who died the same month, a memorial (p. 64) to them was erected in the garden.

Of other major architectural treasures it was probably obvious that the General Post Office, headquarters of the Easter Rising, would be rescued given its symbolic importance. It was completely rebuilt behind its original façade from 1924–29. Less likely was that other such structures would be offered a similar salvation. Both the Custom House and the Four Courts had been all but obliterated by the fires and assaults that ripped through them in 1921 and 1922 respectively. Each had been home to an arm of the previous administration, the courts and local government. Indeed the Custom House was chosen as a target during the war on independence specifically because of its symbolism. It is curious then that both should have been restored and rebuilt. From 1924–31 the Four Courts was re-erected and from 1926–29 the Custom House was rebuilt. During the rebuilding of the former the courts were housed temporarily within the State Apartments of Dublin Castle, another potently symbolic structure that fared remarkably well under the new regime. In 1931, on an

13-28 Lower Fitzwilliam Street, Dublin

Here we see the row of houses being slowly demolished to make way for the new headquarters of the Electricity Supply Board (ESB). The

opposition and controversy this destruction engendered did much to bring the fate of many historic structures to public attention.

even stranger note, work began on the garden of remembrance, dedicated to the memory of the Irish soldiers of the First World War, following the designs of the English architect Sir Edwin Lutyens.

1932 saw the government change. Those who had supported the treaty with Britain were ousted after 10 years in power, in favour of a new party called Fianna Fáil, composed of those who had been anti-treaty and led by Éamon de Valera. The new political tone was one of emphasising the 'Irishness' of Ireland and of forging a separated identity for the nation to that of Britain. Fine architectural examples of this new tone survive in the form of the Dublin Airport Terminal at Collinstown, Co. Dublin, built from 1936-42, and of the new Department of Industry and Commerce on Kildare St, Dublin, constructed from 1939–42. This notion of emphasising Ireland's separateness and independence found a political outlet on the outbreak of the Second World War. The south of Ireland opted for neutrality rather than join the allies. There was undoubtedly an economic reason behind this move, as well as a political one, but in the long term it saved the Free State in the south from the chaos of the blitz and massive loss of life. Not so the north. With one part of the island actively at war and the other part actively avoiding being drawn into it, it served to consolidate the relatively recent partitioning of the island. This separateness was emphasised by what it was called – in the south the period 1939–45 being known by the rather ambiguous term of 'the emergency'.

Bar one or two accidents or miscalculations by the Axis side, the south of the island escaped the wartime acts of destruction. The worst of these accidents was a direct hit by a bomb, to the area of Dublin's North Strand, on 31 May 1941, in which 28 people were killed. While the south succumbed to rationing and censorship seen elsewhere, the full impact of engagement was felt north of the border. Large country houses like Downhill (p. 338), Castle Archdale (p. 373) and Drumbanagher (p. 315) were requisitioned for wartime use. The building of the new Northern Irish parliament at Stormont, an imperial massing of Portland stone perched on a hill, was coated with black pitch to avoid it being recognised by would-be bombers. Its position, the westernmost of the allied territories, made northern Ireland the best place from which to patrol the Atlantic for German U-boats. The large industrial hub of the Lagan Valley, centred on Belfast and populated with factories and shipyards, was immediately put to work making planes and warships. Its location, so far removed from continental Europe, gave the Northern Irish government a sense of false security, so that when the inevitable came they faced it relatively unprepared.

It had been decided that the level of risk was 'not sufficiently great' in the words of Edmond Warnock, Parliamentary Secretary to the Northern Ireland Ministry of Home Affairs, to warrant imposing the mandatory provision of air raid shelters on factory owners. Belfast was also short of anti-aircraft guns and searchlights, and there were too few air raid wardens, firemen and civil defence members. The first attack came on the night of 7 April 1941, during which the Harland & Wolff aircraft factory suffered a direct hit. The following week, on the night of Easter Tuesday, 15 April, the airborne assailants returned just after 10.30pm, bringing with them complete devastation. By 4am the whole north of the city was in flames. A telegraph was sent to de Valera in the south seeking assistance. Although neutral, 13 fire brigades from Dundalk, Drogheda, Dublin and other towns in the south were sent north. It was estimated that about 900 people lost their lives that night. It was the greatest loss of life in one single night of the blitz anywhere outside of London. It left the city decimated, its sturdy and elegant Victorian industrial charm in ruins, the scars of which can still be seen today. Belfast wasn't the only target. Londonderry, Bangor and Newtonards also suffered. When the war was over and large buildings and houses that had been requisitioned were returned to their owners, many found them in a far worse state than they had been just a few years earlier. Some had been so roughly treated that, like Castle Archdale, they were completely abandoned by their families.

Post-War
When the war ended, the world was a changed place. Largely urged on by the leaps forward in technology, which had been achieved by wartime necessity, the post-war decades saw economic growth, the spread of technology and the advent of the 'modern' world. Previous concerns about emphasising its distinction from Britain saw Ireland turn less towards its past and more towards the modern, international world. The most visible manifestations of this were rural electrification, rolled out after the war, and the rise of the car. Discouragingly it was also manifested in a renewed disdain for its built past.

The Land Commission, reconstituted under the new Free State in 1923, became an unwitting poster-boy for this new attitude. It continued to do its work of buying up large concentrations of land. From 1923 its powers were expanded to allow for land that was untenanted or owned by non-Irish citizens to be compulsorily purchased. It continued purchasing land up until 1983, and was finally dissolved in 1999. Many of the estates it purchased included a large house, with the surrounding land divided up with concrete fence posts and wire, sometimes running right up to the front door. Desmond Guinness, writing in the *Georgian Society Bulletin* of 1988, described the Commission's methods:

'The buildings were emptied and left shuttered up for years while the dreamers [in the Commission] decided how to carve up the place. A favourite ploy was to run the statutory concentration camp fence ten feet or so from the front steps. The trees were cut, the garden went wild and no longer gave any employment. In terms of national investment it was a waste. The house would be advertised for sale, through the means of a five-line advertisement on the back page of the local paper, to ensure that no-one except the demolition men could possibly be misguided enough to buy it.'

Many of these houses were made unsustainable, sold off with no land to support them – Duckett's Grove (p. 39) was sold on just eleven acres. Some had already been abandoned, others converted to house livestock or farming machinery. In many cases they were simply left vacant and exposed, to decay at their own pace under the constant soaking of the soft Irish rain, like Wardtown House, Co. Donegal (p. 340). Occasionally however, the Commission found itself with something of a gem in its possession, but sadly showed no distinction in their treatment of it.

One such treasure was Shanbally Castle, Co. Tipperary (pp. 224–225). The Commission acquired the remnants of the Shanbally estate in 1954, by which time it had been reduced from almost 35,000 acres at its zenith to just 1,000. Two sisters, Lady Constance Butler and Lady Beatrice Pole-Carew, had lived in the castle up until the latter's death in 1952, following which there was a five-day sale of the house contents. When the Commission acquired the estate they began their work, felling trees from the grounds and dividing up the land, while they looked for a possible new owner for the house, which was in a very good state of repair. Edward Sackville-West, an English baron and theatre critic, came close to buying it, with 163 acres, but withdrew when the Commission refused to stop cutting down trees on the land he intended to purchase. By 1957 it had been decided to demolish the house, as no other buyer could be found and the roof, battlements and internal fittings were removed.

Opposition, coming from the local community, was vocal. It included a slim number of parliamentarians and Denis Gwynn, Professor of Modern Irish History at University College, Cork, who was also chairman of the Cork advisory group of the Irish Arts Council, a government body. In an article in the *Cork Examiner* newspaper he asked: 'What conceivable justification can there by for incurring the great expense of demolishing this unique Irish mansion?', also pointing out that it had 'been well known for years as one of the most graceful and original examples in Ireland of late Georgian architecture'. It was suggested that the house might be taken on by a religious order or that it might become a forestry school, but to no avail. The house was gradually razed over the course of three years, the final evidence of its existence being removed with dynamite. In a feeble attempt to justify its actions the government stated that 'Apart from periods of military occupation the castle remained wholly unoccupied for 40 years.' Those who remembered attending the sale of the contents in 1952 of course rebutted this. The *Cork Examiner* summed up the views of the minority at the time, in 1957, by stating that 'Unless the present trends of the Department of Lands are stayed, there will be nothing in fifty years left to link the age of the Norman castle tower as a habitation, and the latest concrete semi-detached council house.'

Similar official attitudes towards the architectural history of the island were even more vehemently expressed when it came to Dublin. At around the same time as Shanbally was condemned, two large, fine Georgian houses, which like Shanbally were in a state of good repair and in government ownership, also received their death sentence. They stood along the east side of Kildare Place (p. 62) and were demolished despite advice from the National Monuments Advisory Council and the Arts Council that they should be retained. The buildings were not beyond updating either, but just weren't considered worth the effort by the government of the day. When they were knocked down one government minister was reputed to have said that he 'was glad to see them go. They stood for everything I hate.' What made this case even more disheartening was that their site was never reused. The houses were demolished, not to allow something better, or different, or more representative, but purely because they were considered reminders of Ireland's past. A blank wall with a gate opening into the back of government buildings occupies that side of the little square today, a gloomy retort to those who would have had seen numbers 2 and 3 Kildare Place survive.

Episodes like this did much to provoke a letter from Desmond Guinness to the *Irish Times* on 23 July 1957, which read:

'Sir, As the Georgian Society seems to have lapsed, has anyone any objection to my restarting it? Our aims are to bring the photographic records up to date, publish further volumes of the Georgian Society's books, and fight for the preservation of what is left of Georgian architecture in Ireland.'

The Georgian Society had their work cut out. The 1960s saw incomes rise in Ireland and more money available for construction. As the country developed and opened up to the outside world, the office block gained currency as the height of modernity and success. While many streets around the country lost sizeable chunks of their elegant Georgian and Victorian streetscapes to the popularity of the office block, perhaps the most notorious case was that of Lower Fitzwilliam Street in Dublin. Since its establishment in 1927 the Electricity Supply Board (ESB) had been headquartered in a collection of Georgian terrace houses on Lower Fitzwilliam Street. In the early 1960s they announced plans to demolish a row of 16 of these houses to make way for a new headquarters building. This erupted into a huge controversy about the needless destruction of historic buildings as a whole, and of that part of Lower Fitzwilliam Street in particular. However, while arguments raged about the merits, or otherwise, of the ESB's plans, two large Georgian houses, long since converted into tenements, collapsed just weeks apart from each other in June of 1963. One was on Bolton Street, the other on Fenian Street, both in Dublin. A total of four people, an elderly couple in their eighties and two young girls on their way to the local shop to buy sweets, died. This shocked the city authorities into what Frank McDonald has described in *The Destruction of Dublin* as a spate of 'architectural euthanasia'. Over the following 18 months thousands of buildings were condemned as unsafe, of which approximately 1,200 were eventually demolished. It mattered little that the houses on Bolton Street and Fenian Street had shown signs of structural instability before their collapse; it was easier to condemn them all. In these circumstances the demolition of the 16 houses on Lower Fitzwilliam Street was permitted, bulldozed through despite a sizeable amount of public and professional opinion against it.

It is also worth mentioning a similar situation at Hume Street in Dublin, part of which was occupied by students, in 1970, protesting against the proposed demolition of the houses on the corner it shared with St Stephen's Green. While the attempts at saving the particular buildings in question again failed, they throw light on official thinking at the time. The controversy surrounding Hume Street prompted one of the most fanatical outbursts in favour of this kind of destruction. The Minister for Local Government at the time, Kevin Boland, took to his feet in the Dáil and, during the course of a five-hour speech, lambasted 'the Guinness aristocracy who pull the strings to which the Georgians dance', describing the occupiers behind this 'open act of piracy' as 'a group of pampered students' supported by:

> 'A consortium of belted earls and their ladies and left-wing intellectuals who can afford the time to stand and contemplate in ecstasy the unparalleled man-made beauty of the two corners of Hume Street and St Stephen's Green [who] may well feel that the amateurish efforts of Mother Nature in the Wicklow Mountains are unworthy of their attention.'

Castle Lackan, Co. Mayo
So many houses, once ruined – either during the struggle for independence or during the struggle against rates, taxes and death duties – were turned over to nature and gained new inhabitants.

While this type of opinion formed even a small part of the official position it is hardly surprising that so much was wantonly allowed to decay, or to fall before the wrecking ball and the bulldozer.

This 'redevelopment' of Ireland in the 1960s happened hand in hand with, and to an extent was facilitated by, the rise of the car. The numbers of those who owned a car in Ireland went from 52,000 in 1947 to 135,000 in 1957 and 314,000 in 1967. The car, coupled with rising wealth, made life in the suburbs increasingly attractive and affordable. At the same time as old buildings owned by local authorities were being condemned as dangerous, those housed in them were being moved to newly built accommodation beyond urban centres and many others were making a similar move of their own accord. The result was a huge depopulation of the once vibrant streets and squares of Ireland's large towns and cities. This was compounded as local authority engineers strove to make towns and cities more car-friendly, widening roads to make room for dual carriageways. Such road widening came at the expense of what lined them, their buildings. This obsession with the car even led to a proposal that the Grand Canal, which skirts the south of the city of Dublin, might be paved over to make way for one such motorway. Thankfully it came to nothing, but it suggests the high priority that the car was given in official circles. As suburbs grew, city and town centres emptied, leaving them even more at the mercy of 'developers' and property speculators.

One of the lesser-noticed losses from the 1960s right up to the present day has been the traditional shop front. Due to their relatively impermeable construction of painted wood, they have suffered many casualties. Many thankfully survive, largely unaltered, especially in smaller towns and villages. Sometimes the glazing has been replaced with larger panes of glass that can spoil the original effect, but the carved surround of the shop front itself survives intact. However, in larger towns and cities the pressures of commerce have resulted in a huge number of losses. The need to appear 'modern' has meant the discarding of many old and original shop fronts, some in place since a shop was first established on a particular site. They have largely been replaced with plate-glass windows within modern stone or metal 'fronts', lacking any sense of individual character or personality.

As the rise of the car gave people the opportunity to leave urban centres and commute back to them for work, it also reduced reliance on the island's large network of rail as a means of getting from place to place. At its peak in the 1920s Ireland could boast over 5,600 km (3,500 miles) of rail running across the island. Following the partition of the island in 1922, the various companies south of the new border were amalgamated to form Great Southern Railways in 1925, those north of the border later being united under the Ulster Transport Authority. The 1950s and 60s took an equal toll north and south, with large stretches of line being closed as passenger numbers declined. In particular many of those lines that had once criss-crossed the border were scrapped. This has left a whole swathe of the north midlands, south and west Ulster and a large part of south and west Munster without any rail infrastructure, which it still lacks today. Associated buildings such as stations and yards were sold off; tracks were taken up and land disposed of. Some buildings were renovated, but many were demolished.

Although these developments were largely reflected in urban areas, the rural situation did not go unaffected. While money caused such wide-ranging changes in the towns and cities, the lack of it was acutely felt in the remaining big houses, dotted across the landscape. Domestic rates, chargeable on any house deemed inhabitable, i.e. with a roof, caused a great many houses, such as Dartrey, Co.

Monaghan (pp. 382–83), to be abandoned. While some families had managed to hold on to their ancestral homes despite the best efforts of the Land Commission, they were required to pay handsomely for the luxury. Houses were considered assets, and if you owned one you were taxed annually on the value of it, despite the fact that in most cases their owners had little or none of the money that was once associated with such properties. A great many had their roofs removed to avoid the obligation of rates. Good houses were wilfully laid open to the elements and soon became ruins. Wealth taxes took a similar toll, forcing many to pay annually on the market value of their assets, including their homes. Death duties, later replaced with capital gains tax, forced many families to sell their recently inherited houses to meet the associated death duties. Although domestic rates were eventually demolished in 1977, the burden of this kind of heavy taxation meant a slow abandonment and malign destruction of a large portion of Ireland's houses, those that had survived the chaos of the fifty previous years.

North of the border many of the finer examples of these large houses were taken on by the National Trust. But that is not to say that the north escaped unaffected. The 'Troubles', as they are euphemistically known, that erupted in the late 1960s, caused untold damage to the architectural history of Northern Ireland, particularly in urban centres, until their cessation in 1997. Bombings were a regular occurrence, and for the purposes of our narrative did the most damage. They were mostly the work of the Provisional IRA, though violence was perpetrated and much suffering inflicted by both sides. One of the most infamous destructions of these troubled times resulted from the attack on Tynan Abbey, Co. Armagh, in 1981 (p. 316).

Even the Church wasn't immune from 'modernisation'. Since emancipation in 1829 many new Catholic Churches had been constructed across the island. Their designs each followed similar lines, a high altar being placed against the back wall to the east, on which was placed the altar table itself and behind that an elaborately decorated screen or reredos. This sanctuary was to be the preserve of the clergy and was separated from the congregation in the nave by an altar rail, making it the focal point of the layout. Over four sessions in the autumn of each year from 1962–65 the Second Vatican Council convened in Rome. The outcomes of the Council's deliberations made sweeping, modernizing changes to the liturgy – the celebration of the mass. One of these was that the separation of clergy, in the sanctuary, from laity, in the nave, was to be relaxed, even removed.

Although no specific mention or instruction was given about the architecture, decoration and organisation of churches – the 'externals of religion' as the Rev. Charles Russell had once called them – the implications were there and they resulted in the greatest destruction of Catholic churches on this island since the Reformation, ironically this time carried out by the Catholic Church itself. Many church sanctuaries were gutted. Decoration, which had once been thought to encourage devotion to God, was now thought by many a distraction and was removed or painted over. The reredos and altar-rail were, in many cases, discarded at the same time. In some instances the sanctuary was extended out into the nave, to create a 'theatre-in-the-round'. In an effort to break down the barrier between laity and clergy, the physical fabric of earlier structures was treated with complete contempt. In the United States this movement became known by some as 'wreckovation', for obvious reasons. Several examples of pre-Vatican II churches are included in the following images, the most interesting of which is probably that of St Macartan's Cathedral, Co. Monaghan (p. 380), whose magnificent *baldacchino* was one of the greatest architectural losses.

Going forward...

We will draw our line here. It has been a bleak narration, and of course sad, but it is thankfully a description of a time and an attitude that has changed considerably. Although much has been lost, much has also survived. The major turning point could be said to have been the foundation of the Irish Georgian Society on 21 August 1958, following Desmond Guinness's letter to *The Irish Times* mentioned above. The Society was formed at a time when sympathy for Ireland's architectural heritage, particularly for that of the Georgian era, was possibly at its lowest ebb. It was neither fashionable nor popular to be arguing for the retention, repair and reuse of what were considered by those in power, and by a large portion of the population, to be archaic reminders of Ireland's colonial past. In the north, where such colonial associations were not regarded by government with the same disdain, they were kept alive by the Provisional IRA in their choice of targets.

Both north and south the pressure of development also took its toll, whether in the decimation of the railways or the demolition of buildings deemed not worth the hassle of repair. When compared to the inviting prospect of the new glass, concrete and brick office blocks which were to replace them, they simply weren't considered worthy of retention. The great irony is that many of those office blocks are now being knocked down, turning out to have had much shorter lifespans that the buildings which they had replaced. The one at the centre of perhaps the greatest controversy, the ESB headquarters on Lower Fitzwilliam Street, is currently due to be demolished and replaced with something it is hoped will be more sensitive to its surroundings.

While Northern Ireland benefitted from the presence of the National Trust, no such institution existed south of the border, and still doesn't to this day. In the absence of one, it fell to organisations like the Irish Georgian Society to try and fill the gap. With little or no support from the arms of the state, it did a remarkable job. Although it lost battles, it won them too. Its list of achievements is long but includes the saving of Tailor's Hall in Dublin City and of Riverstown House, Co. Cork in 1966; of Castletown House, Co. Kildare in 1967; of Roundwood House, Co. Laois in 1970 and of Damer House, Co. Tipperary in 1984. Perhaps its greatest lasting legacy, however, was the attention it drew to Ireland's historic architecture. It has helped to explain the importance of buildings as products of their time, of their history and of their craftsmen – our ancestors – and still does.

The other great legacy of the Society has been their photographs, and those of the people who began to take notice of Ireland's imperilled historic buildings before so many of them were lost. While the demolition has never really stopped, only slowed, it is thanks to those who had this foresight that we have a good photographic record of much of what has been lost. The Georgian Society donated their photographs to the National Trust Archive when it was set up in 1976, and there they remain, along with thousands more acquired since, in what is now known as the Irish Architectural Archive – from which the majority of photographs in this book have come. The fact of their very existence reveals a lack of care and appreciation, the misguided assumptions of some generations and, in some cases, the apathy of the current one too, when it comes to Ireland's architectural past.

Ruskin once said that 'without architecture, you cannot remember' and this, even more than their historical importance and pleasing design, is probably the most immediate reason for preserving old buildings. They are the most tangible link we have to the past, to our ancestors, to our history – and through all this to ourselves. They help to preserve memories. They are the embodiment of stories, of the people who built them, of those who lived or worked in them and of the events that happened in and around them. They are about as close as we can come to stepping back into the past.

It was once said that for evil to flourish in the world all it takes is for good men and women to stand idly by, and so it is with our built heritage. Unless we make our interest in, awareness of and love for these buildings known to those who are charged with keeping a watchful eye on them (government and local authorities) and to those who would bulldoze them as useless or archaic ('developers'), they will all sooner or later disappear.

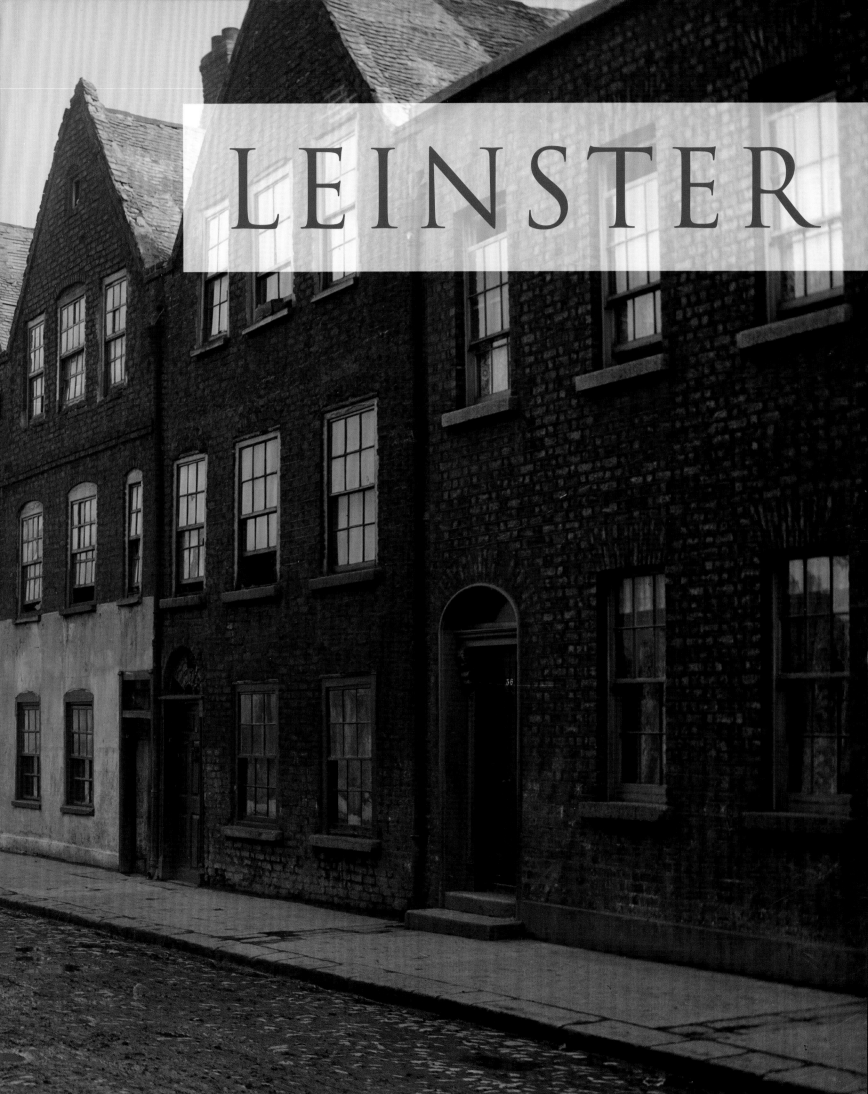

LEINSTER

CARLOW

Carlow was described by Samuel Lewis, in his 1837 *Topographical Dictionary of Ireland*, as having a 'considerable variety of surface ... from broad valleys of great fertility and beauty, rising into low hills clothed to the summits with a rich herbage varied by fine plantations.' It is a landscape of agricultural abundance. It was the ancient seat of the kings of Leinster, whose descendants, the McMurrough-Kavanaghs, still live locally at Borris Castle.

Given its location on the frontier of the old English 'pale' the county was always a tumultuous spot. Cromwell besieged the county town of Carlow in 1650, and later it was the scene of much fighting during the rebellion of 1798.

Of its other towns, Bagenalstown is today the most curious. It was founded by William Bagenal, of nearby Dunleckeny Manor, with the intention of creating a 'new Versailles' here in the south-east of Ireland. This was to be made viable by the route of the mail coach through the town, which, unfortunately for Mr Bagenal, was in the end routed through Leighlinbridge. The fortunes of the town were saved, somewhat, with the eventual arrival of the railway in 1846. Although today known officially as Muine Bheag, many still refer to it by the name of its founder.

As can be imagined, such a bountiful land, as described by Lewis, created a certain amount of wealth, which was reflected in many of its buildings, from factories to churches to homes of every size. Sadly several have been lost over the years. While no hope remains for the repair and reuse of such places as Duckett's Grove, there is still a chance for places like Holloden.

Duckett's Grove was once a relatively modest Georgian house, though on seeing what remains today this would be hard to imagine. Dramatic verticals of towers, turrets and parapets contrast with the wide flat horizontal of the Carlow Plain. All of this is the result of the remodelling of the original house, which happened from about 1818 onwards. It once stood at the centre of a 12,000-acre estate, of which the Duckett family were considered good landlords. Perhaps it was for this reason that the house survived unscathed through the chaos of the years 1919–1923. It eventually made its way to the Land Commission, who stripped it of its estates and sold the house with just 11 acres to a local businessman in 1931. The house itself was mysteriously gutted by fire in 1937 and survives as a shell. It is curious to note however that its effect is not diminished. Although no longer habitable, it still impresses viewers and visitors with its size, variety and pretention. Sadly burnt out, it thankfully still stands today as one of the most picturesque ruins in Ireland.

Opposite: Salmon Weir, Carlow
The Salmon Weir, and Carlow Castle beyond it, in Carlow Town. The small buildings along the water's edge have since been swept away and the view of the Castle has now been obliterated by a haphazard collection of multi-storey apartment blocks.

Country Grandeur

All above: Pollacton House, Carlow

In 1803 the architect Richard Morrison was engaged by Sir Charles Burton, to remodel an earlier house built about 1750. Its relatively heavy exterior hid a light and delicate interior. It was demolished in 1970.

The entrance hall was a bright and delicate space, with fluted columns recessed either side of the doors opening off it. The plasterwork, by one James Talbot, contained the family crest in roundels within the frieze.

The door opposite the entrance had an interior fanlight overhead and opened into the stair hall. The stair was an elegant cantilevered construction with turned wooden balusters and rose, in a gentle curve, up through the house.

Below: Burton Hall, Carlow

Possibly designed by Benjamin Burton, MP and amateur architect, some time around 1712 when he bought the estate from the Crown. Sometime after this photograph was taken it lost the uppermost of its three storeys. When it was demolished in 1930 a hoard of silver was reputedly found hidden behind a panelled alcove.

Above: Myshall Lodge, Myshall

The original Myshall Lodge was built by Robert Cornwall in the second half of the eighteenth century. As can be seen from the photograph, it was much altered thereafter, resulting in a disjointed but picturesque composition. It lay vacant from about 1915 and was burnt out in 1922.

Below: Knockduff House, Marley

A modest five-bay house of about 1750 with a steeply pitched floating pediment in the centre. The house was until recently derelict, although still retaining some of its interior joinery. Recent restoration work has attempted to bring it back to life.

Bagenal's 'New Versailles'

Above: Market Square, Bagenalstown

Like many Irish towns the main street of Bagenalstown was quite wide and functioned as a market place throughout the year. It was lined on either side with modest but comfortable shops and homes.

Several shown here no longer survive, notably the grand three-storey building that terminates the view. Today its site is occupied by Bagenalstown Credit Union.

Above: Lodge Mills, Bagenalstown

This seven-storey industrial complex dates to 1824. Once a thriving source of employment it today lies derelict. While the main block, visible on the left of the image, survives, many of the other buildings don't.

Right: Church, Bagenalstown

The interior of St Andrew's Church, here shown probably sometime after its renovation in 1893. The elaborate decoration around the altar has today disappeared, as has the paintwork in the ceiling. Both were probably swept away in the renovations of 1978 that followed in the wake of Vatican II.

Town Trademarks

Above: Presentation Convent, Tullow St, Carlow

The Presentation Convent, built in 1877, is easily identifiable here by its pointed tower. Next to it, on the right, is the Convent National School added in 1899. The school was demolished in 1993 and, although the convent survives, it lacks its tower. The opposite side of the street has been ruined by an inappropriate commercial 'block'.

Left: House and Shop, Leighlinbridge

This little house in Leighlinbridge is typical of the kind of buildings that were once so common in Irish towns across the island. Its variety of building materials would have been hidden behind a coat of render and then lime-washed to appear white. The large window on the left suggests it was once a shop.

Above and below: Holloden House, Bagenalstown

Holloden is a sizeable house from about 1755. Its pedimented breakfront, with round-headed windows, helps to lift the façade beyond the ordinary. Until recently overgrown and in a state of ruin, it is currently undergoing extensive renovation that will see it open its doors again as part of a new distillery being developed within its grounds.

The entrance hall, shown below, was a fine panelled room. Its decoration was typical of many Irish country houses – the large antlers over the door likely those of an extinct 'Great Irish Elk'. Such trophies were quite popular and common, and still are today.

The sitting room, which opened off the entrance hall, was a classic Irish example of making ends meet. Its sense of decoration and ornamentation would have been achieved relatively cheaply by using printed paper, a corner of which can be seen peeling away.

Opposite above: Carlow Workhouse, Carlow

The Carlow Union Workhouse was built between 1842–44 to the design of George Wilkinson. Its grand Italianate façade disguised the grim reality of life for the 800 people it was intended to accommodate. It was commandeered by the Free State army in 1921 and later the site was cleared to make way for the Institute of Technology, Carlow.

Opposite below: Kilbride House

Parts of Kilbride House were said to date back as far as the 1720s. In the nineteenth century a new, Italianate house was built at right angles to the older one, forming a 'T'. The house, home of the K'Eogh family, was destroyed by a fire in 1927 that burned for three days.

Above: St Austin's Abbey, Tullow

St Austin's was a French Gothic house designed by the partnership of Sir Thomas Newenham Deane and Benjamin Woodward. Constructed in the latter half of the 1850s it was gutted by fire in 1921. Here the ruins of the house have been converted to agricultural use.

Below: Duckett's Grove, Rainstown

In 1830 the architect Thomas Cobden transformed a relatively modest house into the sprawling Gothic-revival castle we see here. It once stood at the centre of a 12,000-acre estate that was reduced over the course of history to the 11 acres it was sold with in 1931. The house was gutted by a mysterious fire in 1933 but is still worth a visit, the gardens being open to the public.

DUBLIN

The medieval city of Dublin would have been quite typical of its time, a rectangular castle with a tower in each corner, joined to a walled town, with more towers at strategic points. Following the relative peace brought about by the end of the Williamite Wars in the 1690s it flourished, the old city walls coming down and a new, more commodious metropolis bursting forth. This was the great flowering of Irish craftsmanship and art appreciated today as Georgian Dublin. It found its most enduring expression in the plain redbrick houses, elaborately decorated within, that make up so many of the city's majestic streets and squares.

The dissolution of the Irish Parliament in 1800, and the removal of political representation to London, could be said to be the moment where it all started to go wrong. The landed classes left their grand mansions and Dublin became a city of the rising middle class, who readily took over the redbrick squares and streets. Some houses continued to be lived in, some became offices or practices, and still more were subdivided and let to those on the lower rungs of the property ladder.

Despite this Dublin's light still continued to flicker, as the second city of the British Empire. This position engendered growth of a different kind, seen in the smaller (but more numerous) houses of the burgeoning middle class. Suburbs, as we know them, spread out around the Georgian city, and with them the architecture of the Victorian ideal – schools, barracks, libraries, municipal baths, trams and, most important of all, railways.

With the dawning of the twentieth century came the great age of destruction. In Dublin the Easter Rising of 1916 was followed, after the end of the First World War, by a war of independence with Britain, from 1919–21. When partial independence was won in 1922, the country consumed itself in civil war for a further two years.

Destruction however sometimes breeds creativity and growth. The great flourishes of Georgian Dublin, Gandon's Custom House and Four Courts, were both rebuilt and restored following their earlier destruction. To its great credit, and probably due in no small part to economic necessity, the newly independent Irish state readily assimilated what the British administration had left behind, notably Dublin Castle.

However, when new independence met with better economic circumstances, it was only fitting that Ireland's new identity would be reflected in her architecture. Hope and aspirations for a brighter future mixed with a passive-aggressive resentment for what many saw as representative of a long colonial past. Such thoughts were given physical form in the bulldozer and the wrecking ball. People and institutions who should have known better stood by, or in the worst cases actively cheered on, as centuries of history and creativity, and millions of Irish man-hours of work, was laid to waste.

Much, thankfully, survives. But much was needlessly lost.

Opposite: Essex Bridge, Dublin City
This view shows the wonderful buildings of Upper Ormond Quay on the River Liffey, between the Four Courts on the left and the Presbyterian Church on the right. The Church was demolished in 1969, and much of the quay's houses have been replaced with apartment blocks with unconvincing 'Georgian' elevations facing the river. A sad loss.

Joycean Curiosity

Above and right: Turkish Baths, Lincoln Place, Dublin City

The Turkish and Warm Baths opened in 1860 and provided one of the most whimsical punctuations to Dublin's streetscapes, complete with massive Moorish dome and soaring chimneystack. In *Ulysses*, Joyce describes how Leopold Bloom '...walked cheerfully towards the mosque of the baths. Remind you of a mosque redbaked bricks, the minarets.' Sadly the building had closed four years before, in 1900, making Bloom's visit unlikely. Following closure it was used for a variety of different commercial purposes before being demolished in the 1970s.

Above: Great Ship Street, Dublin City

Ship Street's name has nothing to do with water but was a corruption of 'Sheep Street', by which it was once known. In this image we see a pair of houses sharing a pedimented twin door case, either side of which are two large tripartite windows. These are unusual features that would have created impressive rooms within. Nothing in this image survives, most of Ship Street having been replaced with office and apartment blocks in relatively recent times.

Right: Merchant's Hall, Wellington Quay, Dublin City

Merchant's Hall, incorporating an arched laneway into Temple Bar, was built to the designs of Frederick Darley in 1821. It was a guild hall for merchant tailors and later became a boys' school. From 1908 until 1980 it was used as a shirt factory, as shown in this image. The building survives today but the interiors have been replaced with a restaurant.

Below: Dublin Cattle Market, Prussia Street, Dublin City

The Cattle Market was situated just off the North Circular Road and opened in 1863. It was the largest market in the city, selling sheep and pigs as well as cattle, all of which were herded in through the city on market day, from miles around. From the 1960s it began to decline and held its last market on 9 May 1973. The site is now home to the Drumalee housing estate.

St George's

Above: Hardwicke Street, Dublin City

The Church of St George was begun in 1802 by the architect Francis Johnston and is considered one of his finest works. It was sold by the Church of Ireland in 1991 and later became a nightclub. It today lies vacant. With the exception of a few houses at its west end, nothing survives of Hardwicke Street, which here frames the view. It is today lined with complexes of flats.

Right: George's Place, Dublin City

To the rear or east of St George's Church once stood a small cul-de-sac or three-sided square of simple redbrick houses, seen here. They too were demolished, their existence only surviving in the name of the 'George's Place Flats' which replaced them.

All Creatures Great and Small

Opposite above: Turvey House, Donabate, Co. Dublin

A substantial house built in the late seventeeth century, incorporating fabric from an earlier tower structure and altered again in the first part of the eighteenth century. Its roofline originally consisted of three gables, with the gaps between them later filled in and the large semi-circular windows added. It was demolished in 1987.

Opposite below: Woodlands House, Clonshaugh, Co. Dublin

A beautiful square house built of brick, likely designed by Sir Edward Lovett Pearce, and constructed sometime before 1735. It was home to the Rev. John Jackson, vicar of Santry, who was a friend of Jonathan Swift. It was described by Maurice Craig as 'perhaps the most interesting small house of the early eighteenth century in the whole of Ireland'. It survives, but its situation is fast being encroached upon.

Above: Elephant House, Dublin Zoo, Dublin City

The Elephant House was called the Albert Tower after the giraffe of that name, for whom it was built. It was constructed around 1845 to the plans of George Wilkinson for Albert, and it was decided it should be home to the elephant and camel too. It seems to have been demolished around 1962 to make way for a hippopotamus pool.

Continental Influence

Above left and right: Molyneux House, Peter Street, Dublin City
Molyneux House was built about 1711 for Sir Thomas Molyneux, a well-known doctor of the time, and stood on the corner of Bride Street and Peter Street. Its early date is reflected in its steeply pitched roof and pediment. Indeed, Thomas Molyneux had studied medicine in the Netherlands where he may have been influenced by its architecture.

The house went through a variety of incarnations, at various times being home to a theatre, an asylum and a hospital. This image shows the interior set up as a dormitory, with neatly folded bundles of bedding on the floor. The house was demolished in 1943.

Left: Ward's Hill House, Ward's Hill, Dublin City
A great mansion of the early seventeenth century, Ward's Hill is here shown a little the worse for wear. It was built for the brewer Richard Ward and it is likely that the central block of the house would originally have been topped with a curving Dutch-style gable. Also likely is that the small half-gable, seen to the left, would once have been mirrored on the opposite side. The house was later divided up into tenements and, eventually, demolished.

Above and right: Weaver's Hall

Weaver's Hall was built for the weaver's guild in 1745. The focus of the plain but elegant brick entrance front would have been a gilded lead statue of King George II in the round-headed niche over the doorway. It however was smashed up in 1937. The building was demolished in 1956.

The first floor of the building would have housed the actual 'hall' of the name, where the members of the weaver's guild would have met. It was a large, handsome room, with much fine detail executed in carved wood, including the overmantle. It was once hung with a tapestry by John Van Beaver, which was sold to the Metropolitan Museum, New York.

Above: South Great George's Street, Dublin City

This image of the north east side of the street shows it as it would have been originally laid out, with a variety of modest shops occupying the street level. This part of the street was later replaced in the 1880s with the Central Hotel, which is still open today.

Left: No. 1 High Street, Dublin City

This image perfectly captures the organized chaos of commercial life in previous centuries. Shops are neat and orderly, but covered with a riot of advertisement. Sadly much of High Street was demolished in a road-widening scheme in the 1970s.

Opposite: Upper O'Connell Street, Dublin City

O'Connell Street was once Dublin's grandest street, lined with large brick houses, hiding within them elaborate plasterwork and interiors. Much of the street was destroyed during the 1916 Rising, and the Civil War that followed closely after. Only one original Georgian house remains on the street today. This view shows how it looked from the top of Nelson's Pillar before the damage was done.

Colonial Bastion

Dublin Castle, Dublin City

Dublin Castle is a classic example of the layering of history seen through architecture. The oldest part of the structure remaining is the Record Tower dating to around 1230, visible in the top right corner of the image opposite. Through the central arch can be seen the entrance to the East Coach House. In the wing on the left was the department of the Chief Secretary of Ireland and in the wing on the right the State Apartments of the Irish Viceroy. The room over the arch was the Privy Council Chamber, in which the castle was handed over to Michael Collins on 16 January 1922. The whole block was later demolished and reconstructed with less attention paid to the finer details of the past.

The Record Tower was fitted up as a store for the state records in 1811. The original presses were replaced with shelves and cartons, visible in the picture (above left), in the mid nineteenth century. The records remained there until 1989 when they were moved to the National Archives. The interior was then gutted and no physical trace of its record-keeping history survives.

The East Coach House would have provided stabling, carriage storage and an indoor riding house for the Castle, the horse being at one point as important as the car is today. This complex, as well as its elegant entrance seen here (opposite, middle), was demolished to make way for an office block constructed in the 1970s.

The Chief Secretary was the person responsible for running Ireland under the British administration until 1922. The library of his department (opposite, above right) was demolished with the rest of that part of the building in the 1980s and new office space reconstructed behind the original façade.

The State Apartments were the official home of the Viceroy of Ireland and comprised an elaborate suite of rooms for state entertaining. Several were damaged during a fire in the 1940s including the old Throne Room or 'Presence Chamber'. It, and its beautiful ceiling (opposite below), were considered beyond repair and were not reconstructed afterward.

Opposite: The Irish House, Wood Quay, Dublin

The Irish House was a 'public house' or pub constructed in 1870. It was elaborately decorated with a riot of painted plaster decoration depicting the likes of Henry Grattan and Daniel O'Connell. It was demolished as part of the construction of the Civic Offices in the late 1960s. The plaster decoration was salvaged and is today in the care of the Dublin Civic Trust.

Above left: Christ Church Cathedral, Dublin City

This image shows the medieval Long Choir of the Cathedral prior to its demolition by the architect George Edmund Street as part of the renovations and restoration he carried out in the 1870s. St Patrick's Cathedral suffered a similar 'restoration'. Such restorations were intended to make the building appear more 'medieval' by removing the intervening layers of history.

Above right: Interior, York Street, Dublin

York Street was typical of the many Georgian streets once lined with large redbrick houses, which would have begun life as fashionable places to live. Later, when such areas declined into poverty, their houses were subdivided into tenements. This image shows a house on York Street in such a state. Most of the street was eventually demolished.

Law and Order

Above left: Newgate Gaol, Green Street, Dublin City

Newgate Prison was designed by Thomas Cooley and was begun in 1773 to replace an earlier gaol that had been located next to one of the medieval city gates, hence its name. The new prison was located on Green Street and was eventually demolished in 1893. Its outline and some of the base of its walls can still be traced on the site, which is now a park. This image shows the execution platform above the main entrance.

Below left: Female Penitentiary, Smithfield, Dublin City

The Penitentiary stood on the north-east side of Smithfield Square and was formed around a courtyard surrounded with two storeys of large cells. Each had a strong metal door and a large semi-circular opening overhead, which was guarded by bars. They opened directly into the yard with no protection offered from the weather. It was opened in 1805, served as a convict depot from 1844 and was taken over by the RIC in the 1870s. It fell into disuse and was used in the early twentieth century as a stable. It was eventually replaced with corporation housing in the 1970s.

Opposite: Library, Four Courts, Dublin City

The elaborate library of the Four Courts occupied part of the east wing. Like much of the rest of the building it was lost to the fire, bombardment and explosions that destroyed most of the building, including the central rotunda and the Public Record Office, in 1922.

Right: Abbey Theatre, Abbey Street, Dublin City

The original Abbey Theatre stood on the same spot as the current incarnation. It first opened its doors on 27 December 1904, as the National Theatre Society. The theatre was destroyed by a fire in 1951, at which point the company moved out to allow rebuilding. Its replacement was opened 15 years later and is still in operation today.

Below: Theatre Royal, Hawkins Street, Dublin City

First opened in 1820 as the Albany New Theatre, it acquired the title 'Royal' following the attendance of King George IV in 1821. It was rebuilt following a fire in 1897 and was known as the Theatre Royal Hippodrome. This building was replaced in 1935 with a handsome Art Deco structure which continued until 1962 when it closed. It was subsequently demolished and replaced by the 12 grim storeys of Hawkins House, which still occupy the site today.

On the Stage

Above: Tivoli Theatre, Burgh Quay, Dublin City

The theatre was originally known as the Grand Lyric Hall, becoming the Lyric Theatre of Varieties in 1829 and the Tivoli Theatre in 1901. It closed in 1928 and served as a home to the *Irish Press* newspaper group until they sold it in 1995. The building has since been replaced by a dull office block.

'Dutch Billys'

Above right: Longford Street, Dublin City

A pair of 'Dutch Billys' or Dutch-gabled houses is visible in the middle of Longford Street. They were built about 1728, as a pair, and would have shared a giant structural chimneystack for support. Maurice Craig described them as being the only unaltered examples of such houses left in the early 1950s. They were demolished around 1965.

Below right: Ward's Hill, Dublin City

Several more Dutch gables on the corner of Ward's Hill. Here you get a great impression of the elegance and dynamism of these gables, which once were widespread.

Opposite above left: Ward's Hill, Dublin City

What Peter Walsh described as a 'Siamese gable' is visible here, again at Ward's Hill. Two simple pointed gables meet and are joined by a gentle dip that bridges the gap between them. Perhaps it was originally one house. Another tentative glimpse of the playful variety of these types of houses.

Opposite above right: House, Pimlico, Dublin City

A much-altered example of the Dutch Billy. Originally there would have been three openings on each of the three main floors, and probably a single opening in the top of the gable. An enlarged window on the ground level shows its conversion to a shop at some point.

Opposite below: Weaver's Square, Dublin City

Nothing shown here now remains of Weaver's Square, which took its name from the cloth industries established there, mostly by immigrant French Huguenots and other Protestant refugees from continental Europe.

Dublin's Smallest Square

Above and left: Nos 2 & 3 Kildare Place, Dublin City

These two grand mansions stood on the east side of Kildare Place. They were attributed to the architect Richard Castle and dated to 1750. The small square originally consisted of four houses. The one to the south was removed to allow for the Church of Ireland Training College in the 1880s and the one to the north was demolished to make way for the National Museum in the 1890s. The remaining two were impressively decorated within, and considered in good repair when they were demolished in 1957, by the government, which owned both.

Below: Church of Ireland Training College, Kildare Place, Dublin City

The Training College of the Church of Ireland was begun in 1886 to the designs of Thomas Newenham Deane and steadily added to over the following years, including by his son Thomas Manly Deane. The large red-brick Victorian complex went on to become offices before being demolished in 1970 to make way for Agriculture House, which still occupies the site today.

Post-Independence

Above: Collins and Griffith Cenotaph, Leinster House, Dublin City
A temporary memorial to two of the leaders of the Irish Free State who died in its infancy, both in August of 1922. It was a temporary marker, of wood and plaster, covered in cement, with the round plaques painted to look like bronze. The designer was one George Atkinson, the first head of the National College of Art and Design. The monument was eventually replaced in the 1950s.

Opposite: O'Connell Street Bridge, Dublin City
O'Connell Street bridge is seen here as decorated for Irish Civic Week in 1927. The week consisted of a series of events designed to encourage civic pride. Like the memorial above it gives an insight into the effort that went into structures that were never intended to last any sizeable period of time.

KILDARE

The wide flat plains of Kildare fall away to the west of the Wicklow mountains and are well drained by a collection of rivers that slice across the landscape, among them the Barrow, the Boyne and the Liffey. Its pastoral expanse and proximity to Dublin made it an important resource in the neighbourhood of the capital, in particular the large open commons of 5,000 acres known as the Curragh.

The name 'Curragh' comes from the Gaelic meaning 'place of the running horse' and it was used for chariot races as far back as ancient times. Today it is home to two of racing's most famous courses at the Curragh itself, and at nearby Punchestown. The first races in modern times were held in 1727 at the former, and in 1850 at the latter. The horse has a special place in Ireland, and horse racing provided an entertainment that transcended all classes and walks of life. Its history reflected the times. The Punchestown meeting was cancelled for the years 1919 and 1920 as the War of Independence raged. It met again in 1921, and in 1922 the Viceroy's car, a Crossley Saloon, was stolen by armed men. It was cancelled during the years of the 'Emergency' (1941–43) but today the meeting continues to take place and has grown into a large festival held every April. Sadly the stands, visible in the photograph on the opposite page, have since been replaced with a more modern viewing platform.

This open plain was also an important mustering point for armies before battle, and saw gatherings of men during the Williamite wars and the rebellion of 1798. This association with the military continued over the centuries. The area was used for training soldiers during Napoleonic times leading to the development of the first permanent military structures there in 1855, facilitating the preparation of soldiers for the Crimean War. It was the scene of the famous 'Curragh Mutiny' of March 1914, when officers of the army threatened to resign if ordered to suppress opposition to Home Rule in Ulster. During the Rising of 1916 all the telegraph lines out of Dublin were cut by the rebels, with the exception of that to the Curragh Camp. This oversight meant that reinforcements arrived much sooner to the capital and the rebellion was shorter-lived.

The Army Curragh Camp was handed over to the forces of the Irish Free State in May of 1922. Under the Free State it took on the added function of a place of internment. During the 'Emergency' many dissident republicans and captured soldiers, both Allied and Axis, spent part of the war here. Its military function continues and today it is a training centre for the Irish Defence Forces.

Opposite: The Punchestown Races
The Punchestown Races were one of the highlights of the social season. This image gives a great insight into the crowded excitement they occasioned. In the background you can see one of the old stands, likely an iron-framed construction. They have long since disappeared.

Military Training

Above: The Army Curragh Camp

Soldiers are here formed into a defensive hollow square, those kneeling holding their bayonets pointed out and those standing behind armed and ready to fire. This kind of formation was used to defend against cavalry charges, made famous during the Napoleonic Wars at places such as Waterloo.

Right: The East Church, Army Curragh Camp

One of an identical pair of wooden churches built on the camp east and west of the main clock tower, from where the picture was taken. The Catholic one was known simply as the East Church and was dedicated to St Brigid, the Protestant one dedicated to St Paul and known as the West Church. The East Church was destroyed by fire in 1923, the west one later succumbed to dry rot in the 1940s.

Army Life

The Men's Quarters, Army Curragh Camp
Rows of small wooden clapboard houses, almost huts, with central brick chimneys provided accommodation for those stationed at the camp in its earlier years, this image (opposite above) dating from 1868.

The camp was set up primarily to provide training for newly-recruited soldiers, which meant learning and then practicing. Tents were an important part of military life and below you can see them spread out on the open plain of the Curragh.

To the left a soldier relaxes outside his pitched tent, surrounded by various items of leisure, notably his bicycle and a cricket bat and ball. While such things provided a happy distraction during training, there would have been little time for them during the grim reality of war.

Gentlemen Farmers

Left: Mount Ophelia, Athy

Also known as Mount Offaly, this large plain house was enlivened by its proportions and its robustly carved door case, which featured a baseless pediment. The chimney stacks and extra bay to the right point to an extension at some time in its past, a common occurance.

Below: Corbally House, Taghadoe

A pretty and well-composed little house, typical of the Irish farmstead with its buildings arranged on either side of it.

Opposite: Belan House Stables, Ballitore

Very little survives of the once grand mansion of Belan House. It was built in 1743, possibly to the design of Richard Castle, for John Stratford, later the 1st Earl of Aldborough. It was a large structure, 11 bays long, and was abandoned by the family when they fell on hard times in the latter part of the nineteenth century. The stables, themselves in ruins, are the best indication of the grandeur of the house they once served.

Classical Conceits

Above: Hortland House, Kilcock
Built to the design of Richard Castle in 1748 for the Archbishop of Tuam, Josiah Hort. It was a beautifully balanced house.

Middle: Rosetown House, Kildare
A typical middle-sized house, added to and extended to at later dates. Notice the Palladian conceit of curved wings screening the agricultural outbuildings. Although still extant, it gives a great idea of how the refined principles of classical architecture were interpreted in the vernacular tradition across the island.

Below: Canal House, Sandymount
A classic example of the Georgian vernacular – plain and simple. A floating pediment with a small, curved window and a simple, solid door case provide just enough to enliven and give focus to an otherwise plain façade. Typical of many buildings of this type which have been lost.

Opposite: Mullaboden House, Ballymore Eustace
Mullaboden was a fanciful Italianate confection with a campanile-like central tower featuring a balcony. The house was burnt out in February of 1923 following which a portion of it was partially reconstructed.

Left: Main Street, Naas

This elaborate wooden shopfront is a great example of the kind of work that adorned many shops in the late nineteenth and early twentieth centuries across the island. The necessity of breaking the pediment to accommodate the overhead window only adds to its animation and reflects the ingenuity of the craftsmen. Many such adornments are the first thing that disappear when efforts are made at modernization.

Below: Leigh's Bar, Ballitore

Shops and pubs began life as a simple room in someone's house. Leigh's shows how a shopfront would eventually developed within the façade – originally a door with a window next to it, and over time some plaster adornments added to advertise what it was.

Stylish Industry

Above: Punchestown Racecourse

The stands at the racecourse exemplify the Victorian marriage of industry and style. The iron frames, which were put together and repeated to form the viewing stand, could easily have created a monotonous feeling, but small details such as the trellis-like panels along the front help to alleviate the boredom. The stands have long since gone.

KILKENNY

The family of Butler, with others like Fitzgerald and Guinness, has had one of the most formative influences on Ireland over the last nine centuries. They arrived with the Normans bearing the name of Walter. Following Theobald Walter's appointment as ceremonial cup-bearer to John, Lord of Ireland (later King John), the son of Henry II, they adopted the name of Butler. They were created Earls (later Marquesses and Dukes) of Ormond and amassed great power and influence, which they exercised from their stronghold at Kilkenny Castle. The castle was home to the Ormonds from 1391 until 1935 and still presents an impressive sight on the banks of the Nore today. It has been recently restored by the Office of Public Works and is open to the public.

Perhaps the greatest scion of this dynasty was James, 12th Earl and later 1st Duke of Ormond. He was commander of the Royalist forces in Ireland during the time of Charles I and, after the Cromwellian conquest, followed Charles II into exile in Europe. Maurice Craig memorably ascribes the moment when he returned to Ireland as being the moment the ripple of the Renaissance finally lapped its shore. The Duke had spent 11 years with the itinerant court in exile, travelling through France, Germany and northern Europe. He returned a man of great power, wealth and ideas. His lasting architectural monument is the quad of buildings that form the Royal Hospital at Kilmainham, a retirement home for veteran soldiers modelled on Les Invalides, which he had seen in Paris. This was the first properly classical building to appear in Ireland.

The Renaissance, which had arrived with the Duke, would later be refined and refracted throughout the island. Many fine examples dot the Kilkenny countryside, the most admirable example of which, in these pages, is Desart Court. Desart was built in the 1730s for John Cuffe, 1st Lord Desart, possibly to the designs of Sir Edward Lovett Pearce. It was a house of perfect proportions, decorated inside with subtle yet sumptuous scrolling rococo plasterwork. Had it not disappeared it would rightly be considered one of Ireland's greatest houses today. But disappear it did. It made its way down the family line to the fourth earl, whose widow was appointed to the senate of the newly formed Irish state in 1922. The dowager countess was targeted by the anti-Treaty forces of the Irish Civil War, as were all members of the new institution, many of who were drawn from the Anglo-Irish class in an effort at healing old divides. Ironically she no longer lived at the house. Her brother–in-law, who succeeded her husband as 5th Earl, had taken up residence. It made little difference. The house was torched, like so many others, needlessly and from motivations that could best be described as misplaced. Photographs of it today serve as a poignant reminder, if one were needed, of the fruitless destruction of war.

Opposite: Woodstock House, Inistioge
Woodstock was built for Sir William Fownes around 1745, to the designs of the architect Francis Bindon. Later wings were added by the architect William Robertson about 1805. In the middle of the nineteenth century the house was embellished with gardens, laid out under the supervision of Lady Lousia Tighe. The house was burnt out in 1922.

A Cottage Surprise

Above right: Dowling Cottage, Freshford

One of the most bizarre finds, this elaborate ceiling was one of a pair that adorned the main rooms of a small thatched cottage in Freshford. They were possibly carried out in the 1840s at the same time that similar work was being done at nearby Uppercourt House. Sadly the cottage fell into decline and the ceilings disappeared through neglect in the 1980s.

Below: Chapel Lane, Thomastown

This collection of stone walls, cattle and a whitewashed thatched cottage are exactly what comes to most minds when thinking of 'olde' Ireland. At one point it was true, and many similar houses once dotted the landscape. Like this one in Thomastown, however, most have since given way to walls of concrete and rooves of tile.

Above: Castlecomer House, Castlecomer

Castlecomer was built in 1802 on the site of a previous castle that had been burnt down during the rebellion of 1798. It was a plain square house with a long, slightly lower, adjoining wing and was later redeveloped to look more like a castle, perhaps in reference to that which had gone before it. The principal alteration was the addition of battlements to the parapet, but despite this facelift the house remained distinctly un-castle-like. It fell into decay in the latter part of the twentieth century and was largely demolished in 1975.

Commercial Flourishes

Opposite: High Street, Kilkenny

While this scene looks very similar today, it has lost something of its charm in no longer being adorned with its original features. The shop on the left, with its beautifully chamfered corner reflecting the turn in the footpath has lost its original shop front. The Imperial Hotel has been superseded by a brick building of dull Georgian pastiche. Only details perhaps, but ones that would have been worth preserving.

Above left: 77 High Street, Kilkenny

This charming shop front shows the glorification of the age of commerce in full flight. Designed primarily to draw attention to the business within it could almost be described as decoration for its own sake. Sadly it had disappeared by the end of the twentieth century.

Above right: Violet Lane, Kilkenny

A laneway leading up to St Canice's Cathedral, whose round tower is visible in the distance. It is lined with neat houses and sheds of stone, the houses covered with a lime render. Notice how clean it is too! The domestic scale of such small houses in the centre of a town, and the pattern or grain they form, is fast being eroded by their replacement with larger blocks of apartments and retail units.

Above (all): Glashare House

A house of many dates, and many extensions and alterations, Glashare is here shown in a state of near ruin. Parts of the house suggest a relatively early date, but the big surprise is the interior, adorned with carved wooden detail. This detail is redolent of Celtic and Norse designs, and would have been quite unusual in any home of the last three centuries. The writing appears to be 'as gaeilge', or in Irish, but is difficult to make out. The house no longer survives.

Peacock Display

Right and below: Castle Morres, Kilmaganny

Designed by the architect Francis Bindon for Francis Morres, 1st Viscount Mountmorris, around 1750, it was one of the largest in Ireland when completed. The marble fireplace, visible in the entrance hall (right), was provided by the local marble mason William Colles and was installed below an unusual plaster overmantle of military trophies, topped by an eagle. A near-identical chimney piece can be seen at Kilcreen on p. 88. The house and estate was sold to the Land Commission in 1924 and in the early 1930s its roof was removed and its fittings, including the fireplace, dismantled. It lay slowly decaying until its remains were finally cleared in 1978.

Cool Perfection

Left above and below: Desart Court, Callan

Desart Court was built around 1733 for the 1st Lord Desart, John Cuffe, most likely to the design of Sir Edward Lovett Pearce. It was a house of cool perfection, the central block flanked by curved sweeps linking it to wings, the whole forming three sides of a small forecourt. Its elegant exterior hid a riot of interior decoration, including much fine rococo plasterwork. The image below shows one of two staircases in the house, this one furnished with a vigorously-carved balustrade and its walls panelled in plaster. The house was burnt out in 1923. It was one of the few houses burnt at that time to be rebuilt but was later sold and demolished in 1957.

Opposite above: Kilmurry House, Thomastown

Gardens were an important part of the social life of the upper classes, especially in Victorian times. Shown here are two different design approaches popular at the time, the rustic bridge at Kilmurry House being representative of the vogue for gardens suggestive of the wild and the natural, broadly known as the picturesque.

Opposite below: Woodstock House, Inistioge

Among the gardens laid out by Lady Lousia Tighe in the mid 1800s was a series of terraces, which reflected the Victorian fondness for rigid straight lines and fussy neatness. The middle of these terraces led to a round greenhouse designed by Richard Turner, who was responsible for the palm houses at the botanical gardens in Belfast, Dublin and at Kew in London. The gardens had been let run wild but have been partially restored in recent years.

Above: Woodsgift House, Urlingford

Woodsgift was a substantial house constructed around 1750. It consisted of a large three-storey block, seven bays wide and five bays deep, with a smaller wing adjoining. This image shows it with an encampment of the Property Defence Expedition on the grounds in 1881. The house was destroyed by a fire in 1914, and afterwards demolished, though a fine complex of farm buildings arranged around a quad still survives.

Below left and right: Kilcreen House, Kilkenny

Kilcreen was a house of the late 1600s formed as a shallow 'U' in plan, the two bays at either end of the elevation projecting forward forming the short arms. Its dormer windows, tall brick chimneys and wide eaves supported on a bracketed cornice are all characteristic of its early date. The chimney-piece visible in the image on the left is a sibling of that in the hallway of Castle Morres, shown on page 85. The house was demolished in the 1970s.

Above: Woodstock House, Inistioge

This statue is of the poet Mary Tighe, author of *Psyche*, which won her the praise of Thomas Moore, who made her the subject of one of his own poems. The statue was carved by Lorenzo Bartolini in around 1820 and stood in the entrance hall of Woodstock house, which was owned by Mary's brother-in-law, William Tighe. It was consumed by the flames of the Civil War in 1922.

LAOIS

The county we know today as Laois came into its modern existence during the reign of Mary I and her plantation of that part of Ireland in 1556. It was originally known as Queen's County as a result. Its main town, nowadays Portlaoise, was named Maryborough with similar ideas of memorial in mind.

It is a largely flat agricultural part of the island and always has been. The monks who established a monastery at Aghaboe referred to the area as the 'land of the cow' (Achadh Bhó in Gaelic). The current name is simply an Anglicization of that. Its towns grew up around trade in its harvests, a fine architectural reflection of which was the Market House at Mountrath, shown opposite.

Industry was not unknown in the area. In the mid-seventeenth century a group of Quakers settled in the town of Mountmellick and brought with them industrial prosperity. They founded breweries and tanneries and mills processing iron and wool. It also became famous for its lace. Such was the success of their ventures that Mountmellick was once known as the 'Manchester of Ireland'.

Following the end of the Williamite wars, a large group of Huguenot settlers, fleeing religious persecution in France, established themselves in what is now Portarlington. It had previously been the site of a failed English colony. Samuel Lewis, in his 1837 'Topographical dictionary of Ireland' describes the French language still being widely used at the time.

Despite its history of plantation and immigration, Laois has had a relatively quiet history. One of its more tragic losses was entirely, and sadly, accidental.

Heywood House was a grand eighteenth-century house, much altered later in the nineteenth century. It could be argued that its renovation wasn't a complete success as the view of it on page 96 shows a rather large, institutional-looking block. It eventually made its way, as so many others did, into the hands of the religious. It was sadly gutted by an accidental fire in 1950 and subsequently demolished. Its magnificent gardens, with turtle water-jets, designed by Sir Edwin Lutyens, thankfully do survive and are cared for today by the Office of Public Works. They are well worth a visit in their own right.

Following the birth of the Irish Free State, the county became known as Leix in English, but is more commonly called by its Gaelic name, Laois.

Opposite: Market House, Mountrath

A fine example of a regional building type that has been much abused over the years – many having been radically altered to accommodate modern uses. This once ornamented the market 'square' of Mountrath, but was swept away in favour of a small roundabout.

Classical Restraint

Above: Farmly House, Abbeyleix

Farmly (sometimes known as 'Farmleigh') was a poised and elegant middle-sized house likely dating to the early nineteenth century. The artist Francis Bacon spent time here when it was the home of his grandmother, Winifred Margaret Supple. The house has since been demolished and a motley collection of outbuildings litter the site today.

Right and opposite: Brockley Park, Stradbally

Brockley was built for the Auditor-General of the Irish Exchequer, Robert Jocelyn, in 1768. Jocelyn was at the time the 2nd Viscount Jocelyn and would later become the 1st Earl of Roden. The house was the work of the Sardinian architect Davis Ducart and was a handsome, if somewhat spare design that replaced an earlier house, which had burnt down.

Its restrained design can be seen reflected in some of the interior plasterwork shown here. Despite the animation of the figures, they seem weighted down by their architectural setting. The house was dismantled in 1944 and later demolished.

Patriots

Above right: Tinnakill House, Abbeyleix

Tinnakill was a modest eighteenth-century house of three bays, the middle of which broke forward from the rest of the façade and was topped with a pediment containing a small round window. It was once the home of the Nationalist James Fintan Lalor, and also of his brother Peter, who went on to become speaker of the Victorian Legislative Assembly in Australia. The image here was taken in the mid-1980s. The house has only become more ruinous since.

Below right: Knapton House, Abbeyleix

Knapton was rebuilt around 1773 by a Colonel Piggot on the site of a previous, older dwelling. It was the birthplace of Jonah Barrington, the MP, judge and famous memoirist who had to leave Ireland to escape his creditors. He spent the last 21 years of his life in France, dying at Versailles in 1834, aged 74. His writings did much to inspire those fighting for Home Rule in nineteenth-century Ireland.

Opposite above: Old Derrig House, Carlow

Old Derrig was a simple and plain eighteenth century country house of a type so often seen in Ireland. It was the home of the Bishop of Kildare and Leighlin, James Doyle, a close ally of Daniel O'Connell in his fight for Catholic emancipation. It no longer survives.

Opposite below: Dunmore House, Durrow

Dunmore was a house of the early 1700s, with a baseless pediment lending focus to an otherwise gaunt elevation. Its quoins and contiguous pavilions with steeply pitched roofs are also typical of its early date. It was a ruin by the late 1970s and has since been demolished.

The Urbane Countryside

Opposite: Heywood House, Ballinakill

Heywood was constructed in the early 1770s for one Michael Frederick Trench. The house is said to have been designed by French himself, possibly with the advice and assistance of the architect James Gandon. The original house was of four bays, which are still visible at the centre of the late nineteenth-century additions that subsumed it. Despite its awkward redevelopment, the house contained some handsome interiors, the finest of which was the dining room, seen here. Its walls and ceiling were decorated with delicate geometrical plasterwork designs in the style of the English architect Robert Adam. In 1941 the estate was sold to the Salesian Order who used it as a school, until it was destroyed by a fire in 1950. The shell was subsequently demolished and replaced with a new school building, but the gardens by the architect Lutyens still survive and are open to the public.

Below: Arlington House, French Church Street, Portarlington

A handsome substantial townhouse built around 1730. It features a central bay that breaks forward, formed of a round-headed door flanked by side lights, a large semi-circular or Diocletian window above it and a small circular window in the pediment above that again. The house is today a roofless shell, but tentative efforts seem to be underway to repair it.

LONGFORD

Longford is situated at the very western edge of the province of Leinster. It is bordered to the west by Lough Ree and the river Shannon, and to the north the county is overlapped by the rounded hillocks of the 'Drumlin Belt' as it marches across the northern midlands of Ireland. To the south the land rolls out much flatter into areas of raised bog and what one visitor, Henry David Inglis, writing in 1834, described as 'a fruitful enclosed country of corn and pasture'.

There have been settlements here since ancient times. Evidence survives today of the Corlea Trackway dating back to 148BC, reputedly built by a fairy as a forfeit in a game he lost to a local king while trying to woo his daughter.

The county has a long monastic tradition, with many monasteries having been established within its confines in earlier centuries. These can be found in places such as Abbeyshrule, Abbeylara and Ardagh. Ruins are all that now remain following their dissolution during the Reformation.

The county also has a relatively violent past for such an isolated spot. It was 'planted' in 1620, and again during the time of Oliver Cromwell in the 1650s. It may have been around this time that Mosstown House was constructed. It was also a focus of the Rebellion of 1798. The French force led by General Humbert, which landed at Killala, made its way as far as Ballinamuck where it was eventually defeated by the British forces under General Cornwallis.

Mosstown House was a large, impressive, seventeenth-century mansion, once home to the Viscounts Newcomen. Like the county itself it had come under attack during the times of Cromwell, the Williamite Wars and during the Rebellion of 1798. Having survived all this it was sadly demolished in 1962 (pp. 102–03).

Of more pressing concern is Carrigglas Manor. The original plans for a house and estate buildings were prepared by James Gandon for the Newcomen Family in the 1790s, but of these only his entrance gates and stable block made it off the drawing board. The house itself was built in 1837 for the estate's next owner, Thomas Lefroy, to the designs of Daniel Robertson. Lefroy, who went on to become Lord Chief Justice of Ireland, was reputedly the inspiration for Mr Darcy in the novel *Pride and Prejudice* by Jane Austen. This sits well with the county's other literary associations, being home at different times to Oliver Goldsmith, and later, Maria Edgeworth.

Carrigglas remained within the Lefroy family until they sold it in 2005. It was let fall into a state of dereliction and at the time of writing is on an Taisce's list of buildings at risk. After spending time in the National Asset Management Agency the house was recently sold again in 2014. One can only hope it doesn't meet the same fate of so many of the other buildings illustrated in these pages.

Opposite: Newtownbond House, Edgeworthstown
A handsome early-to-mid eighteenth-century house possibly built around 1729 when the estate of Newtownflood was purchased by the Rev. James Bond and renamed Newtownbond. Its simple elevation was given just enough interest by its smart doorcase, window surrounds and quoins to lift it above the ordinary. The house was demolished in the second half of the twentieth century.

Early Building Adventures

Below: Tennalick House, Abbeyshrule

Tennalick is a mysterious construction. The building may incorporate parts of an earlier house built around 1660 for Captain Henry Sankey, who was granted the estate in 1654. The current building, L-shaped in plan, dates to around 1710 and once formed part of a larger structure, elements of which were later demolished. It is possible that that part of the house was originally designed as a stable, and it was used for the same purpose again in the mid 1800s. It was returned to use as a house at the end of the 1800s and was finally abandoned in the 1970s. It is today a roofless ruin, but important for its early age and not beyond repair.

Opposite: Longford Castle, Longford

The Castle was built around 1627 in the town of Longford for Francis Aungier, who was created Baron Aungier of Longford by King James I. The Castle's main purpose would have been to consolidate Sir Francis's control of the town and over the centuries it would have been modified as times became more peaceful. This image shows it somewhat the worse for wear. It eventually became derelict and was demolished in 1972.

Mosstown

All: Mosstown House, Ballymahon

Mosstown was a large house built in the late seventeenth century and later altered in the eighteenth century. Its high-pitched roof, dormer windows and tall robust chimney-stacks are all characteristic of its early date of construction.

Within, the house contained some good panelled interiors of the early 1700s, and a very fine staircase. The images here show the house relegated to being a glorified outbuilding, one of the panelled rooms being used as a potting shed. Abandoned, it was demolished in the face of some protest in the 1960s.

On the Edge of the Precipice

All: Carrigglas Manor, Carrigglass

Carrigglas, as it survives today, is largely the result of two families and two architects. The estate was in the possession of the Newcomens, a family of Dublin bankers, from the late 1600s. In the late eighteenth century they commissioned the architect James Gandon to prepare designs for a house and associated buildings. The family bank went bankrupt in 1825, before the house was built, and Gandon's main contribution is today seen in the farmyard he designed.

Following the bankruptcy Carrigglas passed to Thomas Langlois Lefroy, later Lord Chief Justice of Ireland, who is said to have been the inspiration for Jane Austen's Mr Darcy in *Pride and Prejudice*. Between 1835 and 1850 Lefroy employed the architect Daniel Robertson to design the house we see today, a Tudor-revival mansion of great character and animation.

The interiors, including the entrance hall and library, were designed to complement the revival of Robertson's exterior, with plasterwork, fittings and fireplaces all designed using Tudor motifs. The house remained in the Lefroy family until 2005 when it was sold. It was bought with the intention of creating a country house hotel, but the economic crash has mean that it today lies boarded up and slowly decaying. In very good condition until relatively recently, both house and courtyard deserve to be rescued from a possible slow destruction.

LOUTH

Louth is the smallest county on the island of Ireland, affectionately known as the 'Wee County', yet despite its diminutive size it has an abundance of remarkable archaeology and historic buildings. Notable among these are the early Christian sites of Monasterboice and Mellifont Abbey, both of which are well worth visiting today.

The south of the county is formed of the gently rolling pastureland to the north of the Boyne valley as it flattens and widens, snaking its way toward the sea. As you move further north the landscape begins to become more sparse and rugged as one approaches the Mourne Mountains. Along its coastline are found its two main towns, Dundalk to the north and Drogheda to the south, on the border with Meath.

Of these it is the latter which is the more interesting. Drogheda was granted its charter in 1412, which united the two until then separate towns of Drogheda-in-Meath and Drogheda-in-Uriel (as that part of Louth was once called). It still retains much of its medieval character in the layout of its streets, and in the massive barbican of St. Lawrence's Gate. It was famously sacked by Oliver Cromwell in 1649, an event that has never been forgotten – Scarlet Street taking its name from the colour of the blood that was said to have run through it following the massacre.

With the consolidation of the ascendency class and the growth that peace brought following the nearby Battle of the Boyne Drogheda blossomed, creating around its medieval remains a fine Georgian town of brick houses and elegant public buildings. The greatest of these houses was Singleton House on St Laurence Street. It was built in the 1730s for Henry Singleton, the Lord Chief Justice of Ireland. It was a grand, brick house of seven bays, sumptuously panelled throughout with oak.

Later on both it and the neighbouring building, which began life as Mr Clarke's Free School in 1728, were occupied by Drogheda Grammar School, which remained there until 1975. The buildings were subsequently bought by a group of property developers with the intention of demolishing them, despite being listed as 'worthy of preservation'. They willfully were allowed to fall derelict and, despite the best efforts of local conservationists and a court order protecting them, they were both demolished early one Sunday morning in July 1989. Legal action followed this blatant act of vandalism, and resulted in their façades being rebuilt, but they lack the luster and patina, not to mention the glorious interiors, which really made the house worth cherishing. The modern rebuilding serves more as a gravestone to mark out where they once stood rather than as an appropriate recreation.

The town today retains great evidence of its past developments, from the medieval to the modern. In recent times however, with the growth of Dublin, it has become a commuter town, much to the detriment of its own town centre and historic core, which today are sadly neglected in large parts.

Opposite: The Bullring, Drogheda

A bustling town, lined with plain but pleasing buildings of the Georgian and Victorian idioms. Those on the street corner in the centre of the picture, with their decorated pilasters and window surrounds, have been replaced with pale imitations, structures of a similar size and shape, but of an uninteresting and lacklustre design. It begs the question – why weren't the originals kept?

Rural Idylls

Opposite above: Carstown House, Termonfeckin

Carstown is the almost-missing link between the fortified tower houses of the late middle ages and the emergence of more domestic large dwellings from the late seventeenth century onwards. The house, although much altered and added to, was constructed around 1612, possibly making use of an even earlier tower structure on the site. Today it is in a condition of slow decline, its windows blocked up with concrete blocks and its roof shedding its slates. Once they go and water gets in, its end will be relatively swift. Although not by any means beyond repair, its future is uncertain, despite its uniqueness and importance.

Below: Dundalk House, Church Street, Dundalk

Dundalk house was once the residence of James Hamilton, Viscount Limerick, whose family had bought the lands of the town following the Williamite wars. The house was constructed in the eighteenth century and had been altered over the years, developing into a picturesque villa. It no longer survives, its site today occupied by a collection of new buildings forming the Carroll's Village development and a car park.

Above right: Thatched House, Termonfeckin

A good example of the type of house that was once so common all over Ireland. The simple mud walls were kept in good condition by the thatch and white lime-wash, which prevented them getting wet. Such houses were usually extended lengthways, due to the constraints of sourcing roof members to span a larger width. Here the extension has been slated, but apart from that and the pitch of its roof, the construction would have been the same as the rest.

Urban Commerce

Below: North Quay, Drogheda

Much of Drogheda's success was founded on its docks, and the access they gave to trade. As such they were the main focus of the town. The old Mayoralty House, to the left of centre here, was designed by Hugh Darley in 1769, and later extended. Much of the scale of this part of Drogheda has disappeared. The Mayoralty House and the pale three-bay house to the right are all that today survive, surrounded by insensitive architectural neighbours: cars. Darley's building is also obscured by two of the most injudiciously placed trees.

Opposite: Market House, Market Square, Ardee

The original eighteenth-century market house, sited in the middle of the main street, was superseded by the one in the image on the right in 1810. It was a relatively modest but elegant building removed from the main street by a square between the two. It was demolished in 1987, the site today being home to the local library. The statue of Sir Fredrick Foster, erected by his tenants in 1861, is the only recognisable feature that survives today.

Above: Tempest's Shop, Crowe Steet, Dundalk

This photograph shows Tempest's shop around 1905. Cluttered but organised, similar shop interiors would once have been ubiquitous across Ireland. Very few now survive.

Opposite: Obelisk, Oldbridge

This large monument was erected in 1736 to commemorate the victory of King William III at the Battle of the Boyne, on 1 July 1690. Not surprisingly, given it represented a decisive and divisive moment in Irish history, it attracted much attention and was blown up by Republicans in 1923. The wrought-iron bridge in the background was constructed in 1868 and still crosses the river today.

Above: Louth Hall, Tallinstown

Louth Hall was home of the Plunkett family from medieval times until the twentieth century. At its core is an old medieval tower dating to the fourteenth century (to the right of the picture), which had a large Georgian mansion added to it in about 1760, and more work done in 1805. The various components are held together in some semblance of order with a castellated parapet. The hall was abandoned in the early twentieth century and what survived suffered a bad fire in 2000.

Below: Monasterboice House, Monasterboice

Like Louth Hall, Monasterboice is a concoction of many centuries with a medieval tower visible to the left of the image, a Georgian gothic wing added to it later, and various other additions of the Regency and Victorian times layered over the whole. They make for a curious but pleasing result. When last checked, the house was abandoned and its roof beginning to give way.

Drogheda's Palace

Left and below: Singleton House, Laurence Street, Drogheda

The large seven-bay edifice of Singleton House is shown in the middle of the photograph. In scale it was a veritable country mansion, dropped into the streetscape of a provincial town. Its demolition in 1989 caused an outcry.

The early interiors of the house reflected the refinement and taste of a gentleman of importance and wealth. Their wilful neglect in an effort to justify their later gratuitous destruction is an indictment of all that is short-sighted, selfish and greedy in the worlds of property speculation and 'development'.

Below: St Mary's Bridge, Drogheda

The bustling centre of a commercial town. The stout bridge of the caption title has since been replaced with a bland concrete slab. The large Georgian building with shops at street level has disappeared, as have the chimneys and warehouses seen to the right. All important reminders of past times, they have given way to the pretentions of modern concrete, glass and coloured plastic.

MEATH

Meath is Ireland's Royal County, a reference that reminds us of its ancient associations with the High Kingship of Ireland, seated at Tara. It was also a kingdom in and of itself, the kingdom of Mide, occupying modern Meath and Westmeath as well as parts of their neighbouring counties. It was awarded to Hugh de Lacy following the Norman conquest and he built his castle at Trim which, though in ruins today, is still one of the most impressive sights of medieval Ireland still to be seen.

The county beyond its towns is supremely pastoral, the epitome of the 'green and pleasant land' of marketing brochures. The landscape is dotted with dwellings that range from the modest farmhouse to the palatial mansion, the most palatial of which was once Summerhill.

The title of 'Royal County' took on a decidedly different tone in February of 1897 with the arrival in Ireland of Elizabeth, Empress of Austria and Queen of Hungary, Croatia and Bohemia, more commonly known as Sisi. The Empress, unhappily married to Franz Joseph I, spent much of her life travelling and came to Ireland in search of its good hunting, as well as to escape the constraints of court life in Vienna. Although a private and informal visit, she was greeted by cheering crowds waving flags and banners almost everywhere she went. She took up residence at Summerhill House, near Kilcock, from where she rode out with the Ward Union, Royal Meath and Kildare hunts almost daily.

Summerhill was built in the early 1730s for Hercules Langford Rowley. It was a house truly deserving of the description 'vast' and has been attributed to Sir Edward Lovett Pearce and Richard Castle, who may have completed the building. Later Robert Adam was engaged to provide designs for the interiors. When the Empress took up residence special arrangements were made. One room was converted into a Catholic Chapel and a telegraph machine was installed to enable her to keep in touch with her husband in Vienna. In between her hunting she dined out with the local gentry, including at Heywood House (p. 96).

She returned again the next year, 1880, staying for over a month. She later described her time in Ireland as one of the happiest in her life, writing that 'the great charm of Ireland is that there are no Royal Highnesses.' This did not stop the population welcoming her as such, and with rising political tensions the contrast of local opinions regarding the Catholic Empress of Austria and the Protestant Queen Victoria was a source of worry to officials. It was made known that it would be better if she did not return the following year. She would tragically be assassinated in Geneva in 1898.

The house suffered no worse a fate. It was burnt out by the IRA in 1921, some of the ruins surviving until the 1970s when they were unceremoniously swept away. The site is now occupied by a diminutive bungalow.

Opposite: Summerhill House, Summerhill
Shown here, one of the large tower pavilions that terminated the curving sweeps or wings emanating from the main house.

Above and below: Platten Hall, Donore

Platten was originally a three-storey house built around 1700. Its design has been attributed to Sir William Robinson, who was the Surveyor General of Ireland up until that time. Less impressive here than its original three storeys would have allowed, its interior was sumptuously decorated. The dining room, shown here, was panelled in oak, enlivened with carved pilasters and decoration. The house was demolished in the 1950s, the dining room being saved and re-erected in a house in Dublin.

Opposite: Loughcrew House, Oldcastle

Loughcrew was designed in the stern Greek-revival style by the architect C. R. Cockerell in the early 1820s for one J. L. Naper. It replaced an earlier house, which had itself replaced a castle where St Oliver Plunkett was born. The new house suffered the misfortune of being destroyed by fire three times over the course of a century. Following the final blaze in the 1960s most of it, including the entrance portico seen here, was demolished. A small portion of what survived, including the conservatory, was renovated as a new house.

Curvaceous Figures

Left: Randlestown House, Navan

The unusual feature of three bowed projections were something of a quirk of Randlestown (sometimes Randalstown). This image, from the yard to the side, shows the 'back door' at the bottom of the central bow. Originally built in the early eighteenth century, a third floor was added around 1780. In 1834 its owner, Sir Nugent Everard, experimented with cultivating tobacco, which he did successfully for a time. The house was eventually demolished, the remains today lie beneath the waters held back by the Tailings Dam at the Tara Mines complex.

Above: Allenstown House

Allenstown was built for the Waller family in the 1730s. It was a large, solid house, which was broken up by the central features of tripartite door with Venetian window above and a Diocletian window above that again. It fell into the hands of the Land Commission in the 1930s and was demolished in 1938.

Above: St. Colmcille's Church, Headfort Place, Kells
The interior of the old church, with its various ornamentations:
altar, windows, and ceiling. It was replaced with a new church
building in 1958.

Above: New Bridge, Navan

A view of the bridge at Navan gives some idea of the character of the town's commercial and utilitarian buildings along its waterfront. Simple buildings of rubble stone and thatch, they would not have looked out of place in medieval Ireland, a testament to the timeless construction methods of the vernacular builder. All have since been replaced with modern apartment and office blocks.

Left: Larkin's Pub, Teaguestown

Originally this would have been a large thatched home, which grew to accommodate the provision of a 'public house' over time. Simple additions served to mark it out including the sign over the door and the almost baroque painted window surrounds.

Above and left: Piltown House, Julianstown

Piltown was constructed around 1830 and displays the more dynamic and embellished aspects of Georgian architecture associated with the Regency period. Within it was contained a fine domed rotunda, with paintings of classical figures in *trompe l'oeil*, meaning to 'deceive the eye'. The house was occupied in the 1960s and 1970s by a religious order, sold on again and suffered a fire in 2006. Today it stands a pretty, but empty, shell.

Opposite above: Summerhill House, Summerhill

The unfortunate Summerhill, constructed in the 1730s, suffered several abuses during its lifetime. It was damaged by two fires in the nineteenth century and gutted by a third in 1922. Just as it was claiming its place as one of Ireland's most important and romantic ruins, it was demolished in about 1962 and the stonework sold off.

Opposite below: Williamstown, Kells

Originally Williamstown was a five-bay house, which had been built around 1770 for the Cuffe family. It was later extended on either side, resulting in the nine bays that make up its entrance front today. Abandoned by the 1970s, it is gradually deteriorating. In recent times the roof has collapsed, taking with it a large portion of the back wall. Soon its fine cut-stone elevation will be gone too.

OFFALY

Offaly lies on the western edge of the province, bordering the river Shannon, and originally came into being as 'King's County' during the plantation in 1556, the King in question being Philip II of Spain who was at that time married to Mary I of England, after whom modern day Laois was named at the same time.

The landscape of the county could be described as soft and spongy. It is made up of large areas of gentle peaty bogland the largest of which, the Bog of Allen, spreads beyond its borders and into neighbouring counties.

This lack of agreeable farmland may have prompted the development of more industrial enterprises than was usual outside large cities, famously the Banagher Distillery. Such developments would have been greatly encouraged by the arrival of the Grand Canal, which cuts through the northwest corner of the county on the final leg of its journey to the Shannon, which it completes at Shannonharbour.

One of its more tragic losses is Ffranckfort Castle, home of the Rolleston family. The Rollestons arrived in Ireland as part of the later plantation of Ulster in the early 1600s where they were granted lands in Armagh. Later members had settled in Tipperary by the end of that century, but it was eventually Ffranckfort Castle, through a marriage in 1740, that became their home.

At its heart was a medieval castle said to have been built for the O'Carrolls. By 1666 it was in the ownership of a Mr Thomas Franks. During the eighteenth and nineteenth centuries the castle was added to and altered to create a three storey castellated house and home. Its chief curiosity was its layout, lying at the heart of a bawn or enclosure, surrounded by a moat and fortified wall.

One visitor described it in 1908 as 'a veritable moated grange... a mansion of the olden times, and one so secluded that few would ever find it.'

The house was sold out of the family in 1910, eventually making its way to the Land Commission. It was bought by the monks of Mount St. Joseph who dismantled it in the 1930s and used the stone to make additions to their monastery. The most substantial survival from it is a small round gate lodge with gently pointed windows and a conical roof known locally as 'the Inkpot'.

Opposite: Leap Castle, Coolderry

The castle at Leap may date back to the fifteenth century. It was extended around 1750 with the addition of two wings placed either side of the old tower. These were given battlements and pointed windows to help link them stylistically with the older part of the building. It is reputedly the most haunted house in Ireland. Burnt out in 1922, it is currently being slowly restored by its present owner.

Cuban Delight

Above and right: Cuba Court, Banagher

Cuba Court was constructed in the early eighteenth century for the Fraser Family. It was an assured and accomplished piece of architecture for the time, forming a large 'U' in plan. The doorcase on the west elevation is inspired by the work of Michelangelo, which was interpreted by Sir John Vanbrugh at King's Weston in Bristol. It became a school in the nineteenth century and was dismantled in 1946. Today it is a ruin, and a sad loss to the architecture of the county and of the country.

Right: Ballyburly, Edenderry

Ballyburly was, appropriately, a large robust and burly house constructed in the late 1600s or early 1700s for the Wakely family. Its steep, high roof and large pediment show a continental influence, fashionable at the time. It would not look out of place in Holland. It was destroyed by a fire in 1888.

Below: Mount Heaton, Offaly

Constructed about 1780, Mount Heaton was a good example of a Georgian house in castle clothing. The house's symmetry is only offset slightly by a tower at either end of the façade, one circular and one octagonal. It was given by the MP Arthur O'Connor, in 1879, to the Cistercians, who created Mount St Joseph Abbey on the site. Although the building survives it has lost much of its original character. As a result of remodelling in the 1960s the battlements were replaced with an extra storey and extensions were added to the side of it.

Church and State

Above: Birr Barracks, Crinkill

The Barracks at Crinkill was constructed between 1807 and 1812 to the designs of one Bernard Mullin. The barracks formed three sides of a large parade ground with a chapel closing the other side. It was home to the third Leinster Brigade and would have accommodated up to two thousand men. It was burnt out during the Civil War in July of 1922 and today only part of the boundary wall survives.

Right: Ballyburly Church, Edenderry

A modest and unassuming Church of Ireland building, the stone over the entrance of Ballyburly bore the arms of John Wakely and his wife Elizabeth Lambert. It also bore the date 1686, though it has been suggested that this may have referred to work on Ballyburly House (p. 129) itself. By 1974 the steeple was gone and the roof had begun to give way.

Moated Grange

Both left: Hollow House, Tullamore

Hollow House is situated within the enclosure of an earlier castle. It is, or was, a rare architectural link between the vernacular tradition, with its thatched roof, and the classical idiom, as seen in the detail of its carefully arranged front elevation. Sadly it is today derelict and overgrown.

Below: Ffranckfort Castle, Dunkerrin

Ffranckfort Castle had the unusual distinction of being situated within an enclosure of fortified walls, surrounded by a moat. Two battlemented, arched gateways gave access over the water to the house itself. This was a Georgian construction, with mullioned windows and battlements serving to link it, stylistically at least, with the old castle that still stood at its core. The house was demolished in the 1930s, but some of the enclosing walls still survive.

Waterside Opportunities

Left: Annaghbrook House, Shinrone

An early house, of about 1720, with a later wing to one side. It has some delicate features, such as round-headed, cambered windows. Until recently it was vacant and although the wing to the left of the picture here is derelict, it has today been restored, thus illustrating that no building is ever really beyond repair.

Below: Distillery, Banagher

Banagher distillery was founded in 1873 in the buildings of the former Banagher Flax Company, which were renovated and rebuilt to accommodate their new trade. The business was dogged with bad luck. Despite being profitable at times the various companies that distilled at the site went bankrupt or were forced to close in 1875, 1881, 1890 and 1899. Following the final closure most of the buildings were demolished, in 1900.

Above: Grand Canal Hotel, Tullamore

The Grand Canal Hotel was begun in 1801 to the designs of one Captain William Evans, who had previously been director of the Grand Canal Company. It was constructed to provided accommo-dation for those travelling across the country by barge, but with the arrival of the railways business declined. It was later used as an infirmary and seminary. When it was demolished in 1974 it was the home of the local Catholic parish priest.

WESTMEATH

The Lordship of Meath, having been granted to Hugh de Lacy in 1172, was eventually divided up when his line of direct male heirs ran out. The lands were split equally between his two great grand-daughters, Margery and Maud, and their respective husbands. The eastern portion, centred on Trim, was awarded to Maud, and the western portion to Margery, giving us Westmeath today.

The county is one of lush grasslands and hedge-lined roads, particularly renowned for the quality of cattle and horses it produces. To the east the land is studded with smaller lakes and gentle hills and, to the west, lies the great reeded body of water that is Lough Ree and the river Shannon, both providing a formidable border with the west of the country. Along this aquatic frontier, and slightly spilling over it, is the town of Athlone, once an important strategic point for crossing the Shannon on the route from Galway to Dublin. As such it was the location of much fighting over the centuries in the various wars and rebellions that pockmark Irish history. In later, more peaceful years the coming of the canals and railways provided an impetus for growth in the county, creating ready access to markets in Dublin, and from there, Britain. More recently it was suggested in Sinn Féin's Éire Nua programme of the 1970s that Athlone might become the capital of a hypothetical federally united Ireland, for which its location, almost right at the geographic centre of the country, was thought to be ideal.

Of the many farms and estates that make up the green patchwork of Westmeath, Ballynegall House was by far one of the finest. This elegant Regency villa was built around 1808 to the designs of the well-known Irish architect Francis Johnston, for one James Gibbons. It was a house of refined luxury, the interiors simple but comfortably furnished, and it boasted an impressive conservatory by Richard Turner that ran the whole depth of the house. The house was passed down through the Gibbons family, making its way through various relatives, and eventually came into the possession of a branch of the family known as Smyth, with whom it remained until it was sold in 1963. It changed hands several more times, and in 1981 the decision was taken to strip it of its features and sell them. Following this the house fell into ruination, a condition it remains in today. The portico made its way to the K Club, in Co. Kildare. The great conservatory made its way to the La Serre restaurant at the 'Village at Lyons' in the same county. While it is heartening to see such substantial parts of a house take on a new life and breathe again, one can't help but feel that if the same love and attention had been given to Ballynegall itself, the question of rescue and salvage wouldn't have arisen at all.

Opposite: Market Day, Athlone
The hustle and bustle of Athlone town on market day. The town would have been an important commercial centre, to which people would have flocked from miles around for the market, both to buy and sell. The water's edge is lined with a picturesque collection of houses and warehouses, some actively engaging with the river by opening onto it. Few survive. Recent development has seen them swept away in favour of uninspiring 'developments'.

Above and below: Ballynegall House, Mullingar

Francis Johnston's relatively small villa of 1808 was an expert lesson in the cool refinement of late-Georgian taste. Simple, yet commanding, its impression was one of restraint and discernment. The staircase hall was simply panelled in plaster and the stair itself, though simple in form, had a brass balustrade that held a wooden handrail, also inlaid with brass. During later times some of the rooms were redecorated, among them the drawing room. The fussy excess of the painted wallpaper, the rococo furniture and the cluttered ornaments did not detract from the house, but served to obscure Johnston's original scheme. Stripped in 1981, the house is now a ruin.

Above: Hare Lodge, Lough Ree

This small hunting lodge was situated on Hare Island in the middle of Lough Ree and was constructed about 1814 for William Handcock, 1st Lord Castlemaine. It is a good example of the developing vogue for the 'picturesque' at the time and may have been designed by the architect Richard Morrison, who also designed Moydrum Castle (p. 144) for the same owner. The house would have been deliberately designed to look as though it had been built over the course of several centuries. The house has declined over the years and is today dilapidated.

Below: Creggan House, Athlone

These two towers are all that remain of Creggan House, their battlements and mullioned windows giving a clue as to the main house's original character. The house was constructed some time around 1820 and was burnt out in 1921. Its shell was demolished less than a decade afterward and these two towers, vacant and with their windows blocked up, survive today.

Eerie Abandonment

Opposite: Donore House, Multyfarnham

Donore house was the home of the Nugent family, built on the shores of Lough Derravaragh in the latter part of the eighteenth century. The wing to the right of the house in the picture, with its curious lantern, would have been a later addition. The estate was eventually divided up by the Land Commission in the 1960s. The house became derelict and was demolished around 1970.

Above and right: Drumcree House, Collinstown

Drumcree was a smart Palladian mansion, constructed some time around 1750 for the Smyth family. Its refined and robust composition suggests the work of a professional architect at the time, possibly one Michael Wills. The house was remodelled in the early nineteenth century, one result of which is the room seen here. It offers an eerie insight into the sudden abandonment of similar large houses. Although vacant when these pictures were taken, it is now in an advanced state of decay, overgrown with vegetation.

Gateway to the West

Below: Church Street, Athlone

This image of Church Street from around the turn of the last century provides a great contrast to the street today, and is illustrative of many similar changes in towns across Ireland. Here the street is neat and uncluttered. Today the area is a riot of 'street furniture' and the pedestrian has been subjugated to the priority of the car. The building on the left has lost its balustraded parapet, but the most notable loss has been the shopfronts. Prominent and unassuming here, they have all since been replaced with banal, minimal constructions of steel and glass. Modern, perhaps, but devoid of any character, and contemptuous of their situation.

Right: Woollen Mills, Athlone

The woollen mills in Athlone were established in 1859 and at one time employed over four hundred people weaving and producing tweed. The original substantial mills, seen here, were destroyed by a fire in 1940. Although rebuilt by 1948, they closed for good in 1952. The site has since been redeveloped as an hotel.

Four Walls and a Roof

Opposite above: Moydrum Castle, Athlone

Moydrum Castle was built in 1812 for the 1st Baron Castlemaine to the designs of the architect Richard Morrison. It incorporated an earlier house of about 1750 and its gothic exterior hid an interior decorated in both gothic and classical styles. The house was burnt out in 1921 by the IRA, in revenge for several smaller homes that had been burned by the Black and Tans. Lady Castlemaine, who was at home, reported that the attackers had been quite gentlemanly, and had helped her remove the family plate from the house before setting fire to it.

Opposite below: Auburn House, Athlone

Auburn House was a handsome and well-proportioned house, elevated on a half-sunken basement, with its three central bays breaking forward ever so slightly. It was built, or remodelled, about 1805. The bays at either end may have been added about 1830. The name of the house is a reference to the landscape surrounding it as described in the poem, 'The Deserted Village' by Oliver Goldsmith. The house is no longer inhabited and is in a state of slow collapse.

Above: Biddy Gray's Cottage, Crookedwood

Providing a striking contrast to the other two houses on these pages, this small thatched house of rubble stone would have been much more common in the county. Set back off the road, it would have consisted of two rooms, one to the right, with a fire for cooking, and another to the left acting as a bedroom. The small wooden lean-to just visible on the right possibly housed chickens.

WEXFORD

Its proximity to Britain has given Wexford lasting fame in the annals of history. It was the point at which the Norman English landed in Ireland in 1169, beginning their conquest of the country that left such a permanent impression. The county has been caught up in the fray, so to speak, quite a lot in the past. Following his defeat at the Battle of the Boyne in 1690, James II fled south, abandoning his army and followers and embarking at Duncannon for exile in France, from which he did not return.

Later Wexford would find itself the unlikely centre of the 1798 Rebellion. Its principal towns and much of its countryside were laid waste to at the time, and the memory of battles at places like New Ross and Vinegar Hill lives on today. It is surprising given this history, and the fact that a small part of Enniscorthy rose in 1916, that during the struggle for Irish Independence and the Civil War more damage was not done.

In total only nine houses of the landed gentry were 'fired' during the period 1919–23. This compares pretty favourably with a nationwide total of almost three hundred. Of them, it has been remarked that perhaps some of those set alight are better appreciated today as picturesque ruins. Somewhat unfairly included in this category is the great shell of Castleboro House on the banks of the Forestalstown River (pp. 154–55).

Castleboro had been built about 1770 by Robert Carew, whose son was to become the 1st Baron Carew. By 1923 it had been gutted by fire once already. In 1840 all but one wing of the first house succumbed to flames and the house was subsequently rebuilt to the designs of the architect Daniel Robertson. Undoubtedly impressive, if a little overwrought, what it lacked in finesse was much mitigated by its situation, positioned atop a grand sequence of terraces rising up from the river.

By 1923, the political unrest in Ireland had persuaded the 3rd Baron Carew and his wife to move to England. Seeing this as, perhaps, a longer-term solution, they had sold off a large part of the contents of Castleboro in a five-day sale in 1921. In February 1923, what the Carews had anticipated came to pass. The rebels arrived some time after nine o'clock at night, obtained keys from the farm steward, and helped themselves to hay and barrels of paraffin from the farm yard. The hay was soaked in paraffin and scattered throughout the largely empty rooms of the house and the whole lot set alight. The newspaper *The People* reported the attack, remarking that all that now remained of one of the finest houses in Leinster were 'smoke begrimed roofless walls and a heap of debris'. Almost a century has seen the house gradually taken over by nature, and it is regarded today as one of the most picturesque ruins in Ireland.

Opposite: Long Cars, Gorey
Long cars such as these were popular forms of transport in the late nineteenth and early twentieth centuries. Note the cleanliness of the street.

Mercantile Exposure

Opposite: J.J. Hearne, Court Street, Enniscorthy

The shop is now gone, as is its painted lettering overhead. The building still survives, however. The keystone, visible over the archway to the right, is inscribed with the date 1870.

Above: M.R. Moran General Hardware, Castle Street, Enniscorthy

Nothing survives of this elegant and simple shop front, made interesting by its cluttered display and stylish painted lettering.

Right: Home and Colonial Stores, Weafer Street, Enniscorthy

The Home and Colonial Stores were a staple of most towns in the late nineteenth and early twentieth centuries. The firm had been formed in 1883 and by the 1930s it had over three thousand branches. This branch is typical of the store's handsome advertising: noticeable and attractive, but also ordered and elegant.

Wexford Town

Above: Bridge, Ferrycarrig

The old bridge, depicted here, was completed in 1844 to span a body of water known as 'the Deeps' that lies between Enniscorthy and Ferrycarrig. The original bridge was a timber trestle construction. It was replaced with a work of reinforced concrete in 1915.

Below: Courthouse, Commercial Quay, Wexford

Shown here is the old Wexford County Court House. It was completed in 1807 to the designs of the architect Richard Morrison and was later enlarged in 1862. It 1922 it was burnt out, following which it was demolished. No trace of it survives.

Opposite above: Bull Ring, Wexford

The Bull Ring takes its name for the past sport of bull-baiting. In the 1600s and 1700s this was a popular spectacle that happened twice a year. The two single storey buildings, to the right of the image, were erected in the 1870s as a new market place. The range of buildings to the left of the image, with curved gables and likely of some age, have since been swept away.

Opposite below: Green Street, Wexford

It is hard to believe nowadays, but this streetscape would once have been quite representative of most Irish towns, lined as it was with simple houses made of local materials. A closer look reveals a variety of differences between the various structures, some having discreet upper-floor windows peeking out from underneath the thatch eaves. Some are wider and some are narrower, reflecting the circumstances of those who built them. Green Street is not recognisable from this image and, to my knowledge, no such collection of similar houses survives anywhere in Ireland today.

Pastoral Delights

Opposite above: Coolbawn House, Enniscorthy

Coolbawn was designed by Frederick Darley the younger, and built in the 1830s for one Francis Bruen. The house was a riot of Tudor revival, adorned with gables and chimneys, and with pinnacles rising up from multiple points. The house was also set in beautifully landscaped gardens, visible here. Sadly it met its end in the Civil War, being burnt out in 1923. The overgrown ruin survives.

Opposite below left: Clonard House, Wexford

A sober house of the mid eighteenth century, raised up on a basement and with an attractive cut-stone doorcase to its centre. It had the unusual feature of being clad in slate against the weather, lending it a fantastic texture. This was once a local feature, but fewer and fewer examples survive. The house is still in good repair, but its slate has been removed. Additional windows have also been added to the upper floor upsetting the original simplicity of the composition.

Opposite below right: Tottenham Green, Taghmon

Tottenham Green was a curious, modest house, said to incorporate a structure built during the reign of Elizabeth I. It was constructed in the late seventeenth or early eighteenth century and consisted of a single storey raised up on an unusually high basement, here obscured by the vegetation either side of the steps. Overhead was a high, steep roof with a grand Venetian window in the pediment. About 1712 a wing, visible to the left of the image, was added at right angles to the existing house creating an 'L' shaped whole. This pretty composition was demolished around 1950.

Above: Macmine Castle, Enniscorthy

Macmine was constructed in the mid nineteenth century for the Richards family. Its construction incorporated an existing medieval tower, prominent in this image, to which were added two ranges, one long and one short, creating an 'L' in plan. It was later home to a religious order and was eventually stripped of its roof in the second part of the twentieth century. It survives today as a picturesque ruin, slowly being reclaimed by nature.

Top: Ballynastragh House, Gorey

Ballynastragh has its roots in the seventeenth century and was built for one James Esmonde. In the late 1760s it was enlarged by his descendent and assumed the form of a large classical house. It was altered again in the late nineteenth century when battlements were added in an unsuccessful attempt to liken it to a castle. It was burnt out in 1923 and replaced with a modern house in 1937.

Above left: Chimney Sweep

A young boy employed as a chimney sweep. Their small stature meant that children were seen as ideal to crawl up the complicated network of flues that snaked through the various walls of a house before coming together in a large chimneystack on the roof.

Above and opposite, below right: Castleboro House, Gorey

Castleboro was an impressive mansion designed by Daniel Robertson and built for the 1st Lord Carew in the 1840s. From the front its main block was animated with a large portico and a variety of pillars and pilasters that spread along its elevation to its two end pavilions.

From the garden (above) it commanded a series of terraces tumbling down to a lake. The interior was equally lavish, as the image of the library (opposite) shows. Sadly the house was burnt out in 1923, but it survives as an impressive ruin today.

WICKLOW

Not without reason is Wicklow known as the 'Garden of Ireland'. Its ranges of mountains provide an effective bulwark against the expanding city of Dublin to its north, cutting it off from the rest of Leinster to the South. One visitor, Leitch Ritchie, writing in 1837, described the landscape as 'steeped in so extraordinary a beauty, that we easily suppose the effect to be assisted in some measure by an intermingling of the sublime.'

The proximity of this landscape of mountains, valleys and lakes to the capital has meant that the county has always been popular with visitors and tourists, both native and foreign.

Squeezed down along its coastline to the east, the towns of Bray and Greystones quickly became popular holidaying destinations for the capital's growing middle classes and, with the improvement of transport links, they have become suburbs of the city itself.

Such natural beauty also attracted a more permanent class of resident, who happily built themselves homes to take advantage of romantic, unspoilt landscape. The earliest may have been St Kevin, whose monastery nestled in the valley of Glendalough, the 'glen of the two lakes'.

Of more recent construction are the great mansions of Russborough and Powerscourt, both of which were designed by the German architect Richard Castle. Of them Russborough survives today, famous as the house with the longest façade in Ireland, and for its perfection of the Palladian ideal.

Powerscourt was probably the more interesting of the two, and certainly had the more impressive setting. The house was designed around an earlier castle, incorporating some of its thick walls, and sat at the foot of the Sugarloaf Mountain. It was the seat of the Wingfield family, Viscounts Powerscourt who, as well as commissioning a new house from the most fashionable architect of the day, later set about enhancing its natural setting with a series of gardens, still famous across the world.

Powerscourt is also one of the saddest cases illustrated in this book. The house and contents were sold to the Slazenger family, by the 9th Viscount, in 1961. The Slazengers undertook a massive programme of restoration with the intention of opening the house to the public. On the day of the opening in November 1974, fires were lit in their hearths and some timberwork, exposed within a chimney, caught fire. The fire brigade arrived, the fire seemingly extinguished, and all went to bed. It was only to be a short reprieve. Unbeknownst to those who slept some unextinguished embers smouldered on and fire took hold in the early hours of the morning. The fire engines came again, but this time too late. What was arguably Ireland's finest house was destroyed, along with most of its contents, at the very moment it was in its best condition. Although recently renovated, it is still a shell of what it once was.

Opposite: Powerscourt House, Enniskerry
The gutted ruins left by the fire in 1974.

The Tragic Palace

All: Powerscourt House, Enniskerry

It is no understatement to describe Powerscourt as one of the finest, and possibly once *the* finest, house in Ireland. Designed by the architect Richard Castle between 1731 and 1740, and incorporating an earlier castle on the site, it was beautifully situated to capture the view of the Sugarloaf Mountain. The house was built for the Wingfield Family, Viscounts Powerscourt, who over the generations endowed it with lavish interiors, such as the octagonal Cedar Room (right) and spectacular gardens. Its triumph was the large Saloon, a room that had no rival in terms of grandness (opposite).

The Wingfields sold the house and contents to the Slazenger family who undertook to restore it and open it to the public. This huge task was completed in November 1974 and the following day it burnt to the ground in a tragic accidental fire, taking with it most of its contents. The interior of the grand Saloon, with its columns shattered and collapsed, can be seen below. It stood an empty shell for many years, and was partially restored in the 1990s. The quality of the restoration has been questioned by some but the building still rewards a visit.

Great Estates

Left: Kilruddery House, Bray

In 1651 the 2nd Earl of Meath constructed a relatively modest five bay house to replace an earlier house that had occupied the site. Between 1820 and 1829, this house was massively extended and remodelled by the architect Richard Morrison and his son, William Vitruvius, for the 10th Earl. The older house was renovated as offices and a magnificent mansion in the late-Tudor or Elizabethan revival style added to it. The house was approached through an imposing entrance front, seen in the picture. Sadly, this part of the house was demolished in the 1950s to make the building more manageable. Despite this loss, what remains of the house, including an impressive conservatory, more than rewards a visit today.

Above right: Humewood Castle, Kiltegan

Humewood was built in 1870 as home to the Hume Family to the designs of the architect William White. It is truly deserving of the description 'vast', its granite chimneys and battlements and gables seemingly going on forever. It was sold in 1992, following which it became an hotel. It was sold again in 2004 with intentions of building on its hospitality, but the economic climate meant that its redevelopment was stalled. Such large houses can often languish until they start to fall apart for want of an appropriate use and a willing buyer. Thankfully, it was purchased at the end of 2012 and we await its revival.

Below right: Coolattin Lodge, Shillelagh

Coolattin was the Irish estate of the Earls Fitzwilliam, whose main home was the palatial Wentworth Woodhouse in Yorkshire, England. The Fitzwilliams sold Coolattin in the 1970s, and the main house is now a golf club. This image shows the complex of buildings around the estate manager's house. It is just a small clue to the size of the operation that lay behind large landed estates in the past. The buildings at the centre of the courtyard have been demolished, but several others have been renovated as charming holiday accommodation.

Left: Kilmacurragh House, Rathdrum

This handsome house was built in 1697 for one Thomas Acton and was possibly designed by the Surveyor General of Ireland, Sir William Robinson. It had all the characteristics of a house of its date in addition to the unusual feature of a carved wooden doorcase forming the main entrance. The two wings, which sit very well with its period, were actually added in 1848. The house was damaged by a fire in 1978 and is today slowly decaying. It is, however, by no means beyond repair.

Below: Saunders Grove, Baltinglass

This large pleasant house was built in 1716 for one Morley Saunders, a wealthy lawyer and Member of Parliament. The house was set in a beautiful park facing a large canal with cascades. It was burnt out in 1923 and replaced with a new house that incorporated some of the surviving features, like the original doorcase.

Opposite: Bellevue House, Delgany

This elaborate ceiling once covered the private chapel at Bellevue House. The house was quite a plain structure, built in 1754 for the banker family of La Touche. The chapel was added in 1803 to the designs of Richard Morrison. The house fell into disrepair in the first half of the twentieth century and was demolished the 1950s.

Georgian Sophistication

Above: Courthouse, Dunlavin

The Courthouse at Dunlavin is one of the greatest architectural ornaments of any town in Ireland. It was designed by Richard Castle, who was also responsible for Powerscourt House on the other side of the county. Originally it was a market house, and later it became a courthouse. This image shows it in use as a motor garage. Despite this decline, it was later rescued and is today used as a gallery. This image serves to remind us of the sometimes unusual uses different buildings can be put to, uses which sometimes result in their survival for future generations.

Seaside Holiday

Left: Boat, Bray

A boat decorated for the visit of King Edward VII in either 1903 or 1907. The sails advertise a local business on the Main Street, showing the opportunity such royal visits presented.

Below left: International Hotel, Quinsborough Road, Bray

The International was an impressively large construction, containing over two hundred bedrooms, that stood almost opposite the train station in Bray. Building work was completed in 1862, following which it proceeded to have a chequered history. During the First World War it was used as a hospital, following which it stood vacant for more than a decade. It reopened as an hotel in 1935, but was not a great success. It was destroyed by a fire in 1974 and eventually replaced with Bray Leisure Bowl in 1990.

Below right: Turkish Baths, Quinsborough Road, Bray

The Turkish Baths in Bray, as with the Imperial Hotel, were largely the result of the opening up of the town with the arrival of the railways in the 1850s. The Baths were opened in 1859, to the designs of the architect John Benson, and consisted of a variety of pinnacles and minarets constructed of red and white bricks, laid to form patterns. The business didn't last long. In 1867 most of the building became assembly rooms and, in the twentieth century, it was converted into a cinema. It was not well cared for and was eventually demolished in 1980.

MUNSTER

CLARE

The county of Clare sits on a large wedge-shaped peninsula, sandwiched between Galway Bay and the river Shannon, jutting out into the boisterous Atlantic. It has been inhabited since prehistoric times, the most visible expressions of which are the large dolmen tombs scattered across the landscape. These consist of large slabs of limestone supported on several large 'legs'. The best known is the Poulnabrone dolmen in the Burren.

The Burren itself is one of Ireland's most famous and unusual landscapes, consisting of vast, otherworldly fields of limestone. Within the fissures and cracks between the slabs of rock that comprise it grow a startling variety of flora, helped by the temperate climate provided by the Gulf Stream. Its stark beauty was famously summed up by one of Oliver Cromwell's generals, Ludlow, who remarked that there 'wasn't tree enough to hang a man, water enough to drown him or soil enough to bury him.'

The other great geological features of the county, and indeed of the whole island, are the Cliffs of Moher. These vast, stark edifices are almost eight kilometres long and rise to 214 metres at their highest point. Looming high on the sea-battered coastline, they form a veritable 'wall' to the edge of Europe.

That the Cliffs are one of Ireland's most popular attractions today is largely down to the efforts of one man, Cornelius O'Brien. He was born around 1782 in Birchfield, Liscannor. He was elected MP for Clare in 1832 and remained so right up until his death in 1857. He was also a landlord and during the Famine he was a member of the local Famine Relief Committee, which provided work for the destitute, and personally paid for the building of the local national school.

It was largely due to his efforts that the Cliffs became an attraction. He spent large sums of money making them accessible, attractive and safe. He built roads & pathways, and provided stabling for visitors' horses. He redeveloped St Bridget's Well, building a new well house, and provided a round picnic table for visitors at the cliff tops. His most enduring monument is O'Brien's Tower, built in 1835 and standing almost at the highest point along the crest of the Cliffs. This castellated structure provided visitors with a soaring panorama stretching from Galway Bay to the north, the Aran Islands to the west and Loop Head to the south. It is still open to visitors today. When he died his body was laid out in state in front of his house at Birchfield (p. 175), and his funeral cortège was said to be over a mile long.

Sadly, despite all of his enthusiastically built monuments, his own house at Birchfield survives today as an overgrown, ruined shell. It is a sad testament to a man who did so much for the locality.

Opposite: Loop Head
The dramatic promontory of Loop Head, jutting out into the wild Atlantic waves. Just one of the scenic attractions that drew, and still draws, people to Clare.

Beside the Sea

Top: Moore's Hotel, Kilkee

The old Moore's Hotel was just one of the many establishments that catered to the touring and visiting classes. Its long ornate veranda offered panoramic sea views and provided a restful vantage point, when the weather permitted. The building has since given way to private housing.

Left: The Strand, Kilkee

The arrival of the railways hastened the opening up of the west of Ireland. In conjunction with an emerging middle class, seaside holidays became more and more affordable. A staple of the beach scenery would have been the bathing car, small portable cabins that would have been rolled down to the water's edge and provided privacy to those who changed into their swimwear.

Tourist Draw

Above: Main Street, Ennistymon

A man and his donkey look south down the main street at Ennistymon. The street is quite a busy place, and almost every house contains a shop of some kind. The small range of materials resulted in a limited palette, mostly of white lime-wash and slate. The street today is much more built up, and boasts a variety of modern colours, which has altered its character. Sometimes it was possible to do more with less.

Above: Twin Wells, Lisdoonvarna

The Twin Wells are natural springs that lie on the banks of the River Aille. Their waters are rich with iron and sulphur, and they attracted many visitors who hoped to benefit from their healthy properties. To that end the steps you see here were constructed in the 1870s to enable visitors to descend to the Wells from the road. An early example of tourist infrastructure.

Right: St Senan's Well, Kilkee

The waters and the mud surrounding St Senan's Well was said to cure eye conditions and swollen limbs, and to that end the small structure seen here was constructed to add importance to its reputation. Such saints' wells were a common part of Irish folk superstition.

Above: Local Man, Kilrush

Above: Promenade, Lahinch

Below left: Cullenagh River, Ennistymon

When the railways opened up the west of the country, tourism followed. In many cases it was the railway companies themselves that marketed the areas they had provided access to, for obvious reasons. In the west of the country the main draw was the natural scenery, such as the falls of the Cullenagh River in Ennistymon (below left). The arrival of tourists gave rise to the need for guides, who generally offered the services of transport, too. Hotels, too, became an important feature of life, both as a source of employment for locals and as a facility for visitors. In the view of the promenade at Lahinch (above) the Golf Links Hotel can been seen in the distance, built in 1896. It was commandeered by the army during the First World War and destroyed by fire in 1933. Golf however is still a huge draw in the area.

Opposite above: Birchfield House, Liscannor

Birchfield was built around 1800 for Cornelius O'Brien, MP and father of tourism at the Cliffs of Moher. It was a symmetrical house ornamented in the style of a castle. Each corner had an octagonal tower that rose above the roofline and both towers and house were given robust battlements. As can be seen from this image, the house has been abandoned after a century. It is today a complete ruin.

Opposite below: Moyriesk House, Quin

Moyriesk was constructed in the middle of the eighteenth century. The main block was linked by curving quadrants to elongated, one-storey wings or pavilions that faced each other across the front of the house creating a forecourt. The house was much altered following a fire in 1875. It was sold in 1932 and most of it demolished. Two bays of the main house, boarded up and used as an outbuilding, survive, like the last slice of a cake left on a plate. They are today surrounded by a collection of modern agricultural structures.

Above: Eviction, Kilrush

This image shows a forced eviction by the Royal Irish Constabulary of a family from their home in Kilrush. Evictions were a common feature of life before the advent of the Land Acts and the reform of the landlord/tenant relationship. The eviction party, with so many policemen and an oversized battering-ram, seems quite excessive against this small, simple dwelling that would once have been a home, not a barrack.

Below left and right: Paradise Hill, Ennis

The original house at Paradise was constructed for the Henn family some time around 1685. That building seems to have been absorbed into a new structure in 1863. The main additions were the large towers with their conical roofs and the wealth of details applied to things like the dormer windows. The interior was simple and elegant if a little cluttered, in the Victorian fashion. It was destroyed by a fire in 1970.

Opposite: Market Square, Kilrush

Like many good-sized towns Kilrush was home to a market house, once the hub of its commercial activity. The building as shown here, constructed in 1808, is simple and plain, somewhat naïve but possessing a certain charm. In 1885 it became the Town Hall. Subsequent renovations and additions, perhaps dating from this time and later, have included the replacement of the whole roof, cupola and pediment. These have rendered the building almost unrecognisable today.

CORK

Cork is Ireland's largest county, sharing with its neighbour Kerry almost the whole of the south-east portion of the island. It has landscapes both mountainous and flat. In 1847 William Bennett wrote: 'to all appearances it was a most delightful spot, combining perhaps the lovely and the grand, the mighty rock and the secluded bower, the sweet cove and the majestic mountain, in the highest possible degree.' He was writing specifically of Glengariff, but the same description could equally apply to the whole county.

It has had its fair share of disruption over the centuries. Following the Desmond Rebellions, finally put down in 1583, this part of the island was 'planted' with subjects loyal to the crown, mostly from England and Wales. It was also the climax of the later Nine Years War, a rebellion against the English, which collapsed following an English victory at the Battle of Kinsale in 1601.

At the heart of this fertile, rebellious county is its eponymous city. Cork city began life as a monastic settlement founded by St Finn Barra. It was later developed by the Vikings, who appreciated the opportunities its sheltered coastal setting afforded. It became the second city of Ireland, an important point of connection between it and continental Europe. Trade, chiefly in the dairy produce made abundant by its surrounding pastureland, brought great wealth to the city. Cobh, beyond the city itself, became an important port for transatlantic trade, being the first place many ships from America docked when they reached Europe. Famously it was the last port of call of the *Titanic*, before it set out in the opposite direction on its ill-fated voyage in 1912.

Since the nineteenth century both city and county have generally been quite nationalist in their politics. During the War of Independence part of the city was burned to the ground by the infamous Black and Tans. During the Civil War that followed, Cork comprised the heartland of those opposed to the 1922 Treaty. The city was eventually captured from the sea and used as a point from which to restore order in the county.

Not surprisingly, given such a tumultuous past, the architecture of the county has suffered. Mitchelstown Castle stands out for both its size and the completeness of its destruction. A vast gothic revival castle, built in the 1820s for the third earl of Kingston, it reputedly cost £100,000. During the Civil War it was 'occupied' by the anti-Treaty forces for several months before being set alight by them when they abandoned it. Later the stone was sold for building so that not even a picturesque ruin survives: the site is today occupied by a factory.

In the later twentieth century the city itself suffered quite a bit from 'redevelopment'. However both it and the surrounding county still contain much to reward those with an interest when they visit today.

Opposite: South Mall, Cork City

Shown here is a beautiful and stout termination to a row of houses on Grand Parade. The twin bowed front is hung with slate, as are several of the houses adjoining it, and faces a small park sandwiched between the South Mall and the river. It no longer survives.

Industrial Schooling

Left and below: Industrial School, Baltimore

In 1887 an enterprising priest, one Fr Charles Davis, established a Fisheries School in Baltimore. Due to economic pressures it was opened up, in 1906, as a reformatory school as well. Boys, both young offenders and orphans, were sent there, where they worked on such jobs as making fishing nets (left). In recent times the harsh conditions and cruelty they were subjected to at the hands of the religious who ran the school has come to light. The buildings where these atrocities took place (below), are relatively quaint and unintimidating. They represent the banality of evil.

Above: Opera House, Lavitt's Quay, Cork City

Cork Opera House began life as 'The Athenaeum' when it opened in 1852 having been built to the designs of the architect Sir John Benson. It got off to a shaky start and was refitted and renovated soon after. Following the first set of works it reopened as 'The Munster Hall' in 1875 and following the second intervention it became 'Cork Opera House' in 1877. Here we see its long side elevation, its entrance being from the curved or bowed end to the left. It was destroyed by a fire in 1955 and replaced with a new Opera House.

Right: Cathedral of St Mary and St Anne, Cathedral Street, Cork City

A concoction of several different eras, the Cathedral of St Mary and St Anne was built about 1808, repaired after a fire in about 1820, and had a steeple added in the 1860s. The result of these different works can be seen in the view of the altar here. It was a riot of pious gothic fantasy, pinnacles and arches all pointing towards the heavens. Sadly, following the second Vatican Council and the zeal for architectural reform it led to, the chancel and altar were demolished and replaced with a new structure in 1964. The contrast couldn't be more stark, the replacement almost minimal in its decoration, or lack thereof.

Dolls' Houses

Left: Mount Uniacke, Killeagh

The house at Mount Uniacke may have dated back as far as the 1680s when it was home to one James Uniacke. The high roof of the house, with its wide eaves, would lend credence to this. It was a single storey building raised up on a high basement and had a curious tower-like bowed projection from one side, likely added at a later date. It was burnt out in 1923.

Below: Doll's House, Bachelor's Quay Cork City

The Doll's House, as it was known, was an early eighteenth-century house that had once been the home of the city sheriff. It stood on the corner of Bachelor's Quay and Grattan Street. It was hugely attractive, a genuine ornament to the city's streetscapes. It fell into disrepair and was offered, at a token rent of one shilling a year, to Cork Corporation, who saw the estimated £30,000 cost of restoration as prohibitive. With no saviours to hand, it was demolished with the adjacent buildings, in 1966.

Above: Palace Anne, Ballineen

Palace Anne was built around 1714 for one Arthur Bernard. It was constructed of imported red brick and featured Dutch-inspired gables – three over the main block of the house and one over each of the two small pavilion wings either side. At one point it boasted suitably impressive panelled interiors too. The house fell into disrepair in the mid nineteenth century after it was sold, as shown in the picture here. Following this one of the wings was converted as a residence. All but this converted wing was demolished in the late 1950s. The surviving wing is now derelict.

The Everyday City

Opposite: Dowdall's Creamery, Charleville

The creamery building at Charleville shows the evolution from traditional agricultural buildings to those on a larger scale, made possible by the use of materials such as iron and steel. The main material, rubble stone for the walls, was still the same, but the roof structure was no longer determined by the size of available timber to span between two walls. Steel frames and corrugated iron allowed for greater freedom and larger enclosed spaces. This is really a prototype of the modern steel-framed warehouse.

Above right: St Finn Barre's Cathedral, Cork City

Shown in the photograph is the second Cathedral on this site. The original medieval structure (with the exception of the west tower, pictured here and also on p. 14) was demolished in 1735 to make way for a more classical structure, completed in 1738. It contained a Venetian east window and was decorated with plasterwork that was attributed to the Lafranchini brothers. It, in turn, was replaced by the current Cathedral, designed by the architect William Burges. The old structure was demolished around 1865 when the foundation stone was laid for its replacement, and the new building held its first divine service in 1870.

Below right: Patrick Street, Cork City

The statue of Fr Mathew, described on the base as 'The Apostle of Temperance', is still in the same spot here on Patrick Street, as are the four buildings in the background, but what has gone are the details, and with them so much of the character. None of the buidings has its painted advertisements between its windows, or on its gable, and none retains its original shop front or windows. The windows have been replaced with bad imitation PVC examples, while the shopfronts have given way to tasteless and unsympathetic 'creations' in plastic, steel and glass, which show no unity with, or respect for, the buildings they occupy.

Above left: 80 Patrick Street, Cork City

This image shows to great advantage the beauty of Victorian intervention in the streetscape. A high ground floor, framed by gothic arches featuring busy carved details, and overhead a restrained (by Victorian standards) mix of polychromatic brick. Hidden behind the parapet at the top is a small dormer window, lending a touch of the picturesque to this otherwise stern, yet colourful, composition. Next to it is an older building of Georgian times, a little more workmanlike in appearance, but beautifully textured with hung slate. Neither survives.

Below left: Statue of George II, Grand Parade, Cork City

In 1761 Cork Corporation unveiled the large statue of King George II on a site in the centre of Tuckey's Bridge, which once spanned a part of the River Lee that ran through modern-day Grand Parade. The statue had been cast by the sculptor John Van Nost the younger and would later be moved from the bridge to the South Mall. It suffered over the years, to the extent of being supported and kept in place with props until some unknown person eventually toppled him from his pedestal in 1862.

Above right: 7 Merchant's Quay, Cork City

Bowed projection, or fronts, are a common feature of the architecture in this part of Ireland. Although several survive, this example, Meehan's Confectioners, is not one of them. Here the bow is almost a complete half circle! Merchant's Quay has since been gobbled up, mostly by the un-engaging behemoth of the shopping centre that today bears its name. No. 7 no longer survives.

Above: Cornmarket Street, Cork City

Cornmarket Street was at one time a channel of the river Lee, which has been covered over, but in times past it has been known as Coal Quay and Potato Quay as a result of its once waterborne traffic. The large market building on the left was built in 1739, and is shown here after it was redeveloped as the City Bazaar in 1843. The other side of the street took its cue from the market and was lined with a row of houses that had shops at ground level. These were swept away and the site is today home to the hulking mass of the Cornmarket Centre.

On Show

Above and right: International Exhibition, Cork

The Cork International Exhibition opened in May 1902 to a rapturous reception. The Exhibition had been devised the previous year, and consisted of several pavilions and attractions. Shown above is the Industrial Hall and Fish Hatcheries, and right, one of the more light-hearted attractions, a large water 'chute'. The exhibition was such a success that another was staged the following year, which was attended by King Edward VII and Queen Alexandra. Following the exhibitions, the land on which they had been held was donated to the city of Cork and became Fitzgerald Park. Most of the buildings were not designed to survive but give a fascinating insight into the architectural pretentions of the time.

Above: City Hall, Albert Quay, Cork City

City Hall began life as the Corn Exchange in 1843. In 1852 a large cruciform structure was added to the rear of the building to accommodate the Munster Exhibition, modelled on the Great Exhibition of the previous year in London. It was taken over again for exhibition purposes in 1883, following which it was converted into the City Hall. That building was destroyed by the Black and Tans when they burnt large parts of Cork in December of 1920.

Coastal Recreation

Above left: The Fleet at Anchor, Bantry Bay
(see caption below)

Middle left: Admiralty Recreation Grounds, Castletownbe-rehaven

Jutting out from the west coast of Europe, Ireland was always an important outpost for the British Navy in times past. Three ports in particular – Cobh, Berehaven and Lough Swilly – were of such vital importance that, following the Anglo-Irish Treaty of 1922, they remained in use as British Naval bases. The image above shows the fleet at anchor in Bantry Bay, near Berehaven. These bases were like small towns, and provided a wide range of facilities, including for leisure. Middle left is the Admiralty recreation ground, which also included a tennis court and a golf club. The Treaty Ports, as they were known, were handed back to Ireland in Sept 1938, thus enabling the country to remain neutral for the duration of the Second World War.

Below left: Royal Victoria Baths, Glenbrook

The Royal Victoria Monkstown and Passage Baths, to give them their full title, were opened in 1838, and extended twenty years later to include a Turkish bath, then fashionable. The whole of the lower floors were devoted to the baths, with a large swimming pool on the water's edge. A large part of the complex was destroyed by fire in 1859 and reconstructed shortly afterwards. In 1864 it became a hotel, which didn't work quite as well as the baths and was closed around 1900. By 1929 the complex was derelict and was later demolished, the rubble being used to fill in the old swimming pool on the waterside.

Opposite above left and right: Bowen's Court, Kildorrery

Bowen's Court was constructed in the 1770s for Henry Bowen, to the designs of the architect Isaac Rothery. It was a large, solid block of a house that replaced an earlier dwelling on the site. A glimpse of its finely detailed interiors is offered (above right) that shows a handsome, masculine doorcase, but which also reveals it as a comfortable home. The house was famously home to the author Elizabeth Bowen and features in her writings. She was forced to sell it in 1959 and its new owner demolished it within a few years.

Below: Derry House, Rosscarbery

A Cromwellian officer by the name of Townshend purchased a house at Derry in the 1680s, and one of his descendants replaced it with the building shown here from about 1800. The house was quite simple and plain, and had a half-timbered extension added in 1852. It was sold out of the family in 1915 and was partially destroyed by a fire during the Troubles in the 1920s.

Above and left: Mitchelstown Castle, Mitchelstown

Mitchelstown was home to a branch of the Fitzgerald family that held the title White Knight. It passed to the King family through marriage and in 1776 a new house replaced one already existing. The Kings became Earls of Kingston and in 1823 the 3rd Earl, known as 'Big George', demolished the 1776 house and began work on an elephantine castle. It was designed by the architect brothers James and George Richard Pain and, despite its heft, was completed in just two years. Big George had reputedly requested they build him the largest castle in Ireland, and the intention was that it would be used to entertain King George IV when he returned to Ireland following his first visit in 1821.

The castle was set around three sides of a court and was entered through a soaring gatehouse, seen above. This led through an entrance hall to the large gallery (left), which stretched to 93 feet in length before reaching the staircase. With a possible future royal visit in mind the castle contained a 'Royal Tower' with a suite of rooms specifically set aside for the king. In the end George IV never returned. The Kings bankrupted themselves, but managed to hold onto their castle until it was destroyed by fire in 1922. It was afterward demolished and the stone used by the monks of Mount Melleray to build a church. No trace of it survives today.

Before and After

Above and right: Castle Mary, Cloyne

The two images here would hardly appear to be the same house, but oddly enough they are. Castle Mary was built for the Longfield family in the late seventeenth century, with input from the architect Davis Ducart in the early eighteenth century. This house (right) was large and solid looking, with 'towers' or projections at each corner of the entrance front. These featured battered or inclined bases that lent the building a somewhat martial or defensive appearance.

In the late nineteenth century the castle was substantially rebuilt in gothic-revival form to make it appear even more castle-like (above). The work was quite radical, as comparing the two images shows. The whole left side of the house seems to have ballooned well beyond the outline of the original. It did not last long, as the house was destroyed by fire during the troubles of the 1920s. The family afterward converted the old stable-block into a new home.

KERRY

On August 26, 1861 a very special train departed from what is now Heuston Station, Dublin. On board was Queen Victoria of the United Kingdom of Great Britain and Ireland. This was the Queen's third official visit to Ireland, but it was the first time she had ventured as far as Kerry. Several hours after departing Dublin she arrived in Killarney to a rapturous reception. She would spend only four days there in total, but they were four days that would leave a lasting mark on this relatively quiet and isolated corner of Ireland, and her Empire.

From the station she was escorted by a bodyguard of 40 of the 1st Dragoons, and the Earl of Kenmare, to the Earl's home at Kenmare House. The roads and avenue leading to the earl's mansion were lined with cheering crowds. The lady later dubbed the 'Famine Queen' by Maude Gonne was evidently quite popular. At Kenmare she was entertained to dinner, stayed the night and spent the following day boating on the lakes. That evening she departed Kenmare for Muckross House, home of the Herbert family, again under a large escort. Here she spent the next two days. It was reported in the local press that it was her intention that this part of her trip be more private and 'quiet'. It was not to be. People flocked from all over to try and gain a glimpse of the royal personage. Boats were hauled overland to continue the pursuit on the lakes themselves. The next day she toured the Muckross demesne and attended a stag hunt. On the day of her departure she visited the old Abbey of Muckross before she returned by train to Dublin.

The impact of this visit was of immense importance to Kerry. The Queen had given her royal endorsement, and her subjects were soon to follow suit. The influx of tourists went some way to ameliorating the effects of the famine. However the homes of the poorer part of the population continued to reflect the stark environment around them – stone walls instead of clay, the stone left exposed far from the towns, where lime render was less ready to hand.

Many grand houses also dotted the landscape, taking advantage of the views so admired by the Queen on her visit, but of the two mentioned above, only Muckross survives. The Kenmare house in which Victoria was fêted was replaced shortly after the royal visit with a large Tudor/Jacobean-revival house, the site of which had reputedly been chosen by the Queen herself just a few years earlier. This was known as Killarney House. It suffered two fires, one almost immediately after its completion in 1878, and the second in 1913, following which it was not rebuilt. Confusingly, the family then converted the former stable block of the first house and christened it 'Kenmare House'. Adding to the confusion it was later renamed Killarney House.

Opposite: Killarney House, Killarney
A corridor in Killarney House gives a definite feeling of the luxury of the interior.

Opposite above: Beach, Ballybunion

Ballybunion was a popular tourist destination in Victorian times with its combination of seaside and scenery. Indeed, it is a combination that succeeds in drawing many to the area today. Shown here are the remains of Ballybunion Castle perched on the cliff to the right of the image, and a collection of bathing huts neatly lined up on the sand. Bathing huts were completely of their time and they are no longer seen today.

Below left: Ballymullen Barracks, Tralee

Ballymullen was begun in 1810 at the height of fears of a Napoleonic invasion of Britain, via Ireland. It was designed to accommodate 300 troops, though this increased as it was extended over the years. It was vacated by the British in 1922, and occupied by the anti-treaty IRA and wrested from their control by the Free State forces in August of that year. It had consisted of one long block with an arch and cupola-topped tower at its centre, seen here. Two separate short wings stood at right angles to this, like bookends. Only half of the main block survives today, and only one of the side wings.

Above: Lartigue Railway, Ballybunion

Charles Lartigue, a Frenchman, was inspired by the way African camels were loaded with goods across their hump, and developed a monorail using the same idea – two weights, of a similar size, balancing each other across an apex frame. In 1888 the system was used to link Listowel to Ballybunion, a distance of just under nine miles, or just over 14 kilometres. The monorail survived in use until damaged during the Civil War, following which it closed, in 1924. A small part has been recreated in Listowel for visitors to see today.

Industrial Refinement

Above: Old Bridge, Kenmare

Ireland's first suspension bridge was completed in 1841, spanning the Kenmare River on the road from Kenmare to Bantry. It was designed by William Bald, and was paid for in equal parts by the Marquess of Lansdowne and the Board of Works, who each contributed £3,000. It was 18 ft wide, narrowing to 12 ft as it passed through the central arch. Being the first of its kind, there were teething problems, with the road surface being changed from wood to iron and eventually being covered in stone and tarmacadam. With the advent of modern traffic it began to warp and move, and so was demolished in 1932. The new, current bridge was opened in 1933.

Opposite above: Derryquin Castle, Sneem

Derryquin was built for the Bland family, one of whom had come to Ireland as chaplain to the Viceroy in 1692. The castle shown here was built in the 1860s to the designs of an architect relation of the family, James Franklin Fuller. It remained in the family until sold to the Wardens in 1891. It remained in their possession until it was burnt out in 1922. Its ruins stood until 1969 when they were demolished.

Opposite below: Kenmare House, Killarney

Kenmare House was built for the Browne family who were Viscounts and later Earls of Kenmare. It was constructed by the 3rd Viscount in 1726, reputedly to his own designs, which showed in its slightly old-fashioned appearance for the time. The house was demolished following the decision of the 4th Earl to build a new house, Killarney House (overleaf) in 1872.

Tudor-Revival Riot

All: Killarney House, Killarney

Killarney House was constructed to the designs of the architect George Devey as a replacement for Kenmare House, home of the Browne family, Earls of Kenmare. It was built between 1877 and 1878 and suffered the misfortune of a fire shortly after it was completed, though it was subsequently rebuilt. It was a large rambling assortment of redbrick gables, chimneys and mullioned windows (opposite), and even contained a spire rising above one end of the the roofline. The house was luxurious in the extreme, set in precisely manicured terraced gardens, themselves surrounded by the unspoilt landscape of Killarney (bottom). For all its expense, the image of the entrance hall shows a building of considered comfort (left). The house was burnt a second time in 1913, following which it was not rebuilt. The ruins were demolished around 1956 to make way for a new house, known as Kenmare House. This caused some confusion as the stable-block of the original eighteenth century Kenmare House had been converted following the 1913 fire and became known as Killarney House.

Awaiting Change

Above and opposite: Ardfert Abbey, Ardfert

Ardfert was built in the late seventeenth century for Sir Thomas Crosbie, replacing an earlier house of 1635 that had been destroyed in 1641 during the Confederate Wars. It was altered later in its history, once around 1720 and again about 1830, from which time the large tripartite window over the front door likely dates (above). Within, the house was panelled in wood throughout, with a fine staircase, just visible off the main entrance hall (right). The entrance featured a series of monochrome figurative paintings set into the panelling, which can also be seen here. The house passed from the Crosbies to the Talbots, before being burnt out in 1922.

Left: Former Gunsboro Court House, Listowel

This small vernacular structure was once used as a court house and later became a school house. Although its materials and methods are relatively modest, its fenestration, in the windows and above the door, suggest a certain pretention and following of fashion – the round-headed windows have been later filled with gothic glazing bars.

Vernacular Variety

Opposite above: House, Ballyferriter

This small house is a great reflection of the versatility and resource-fulness of the vernacular builder. Local materials, stone and thatch, are used, but here the builder is working from his mind and not from a drawing and so the shape and form of the house dynamically adapt to the circumstances, resulting in something both practical and picturesque.

Opposite below left and right: Clocháns

Clocháns are typically small round, dry-stone huts with corbelled roofs, though as time passed rectangular plans became more common, as did coverings of thatch or sods. They are a building type particularly associated with the south west of the island, and have existed in Ireland as far back as the eighth century when they would have been built as shelters, most famously the beehive huts constructed by hermetic monks on places like Skellig Michael. In later times they were used as outhouses, such as the one seen here on the Great Blasket Island (below left), or would have been constructed as temporary shelters for shepherds on the hillside, such at that at Dunquin (below right). Their predominantly circular plan links them back to the circular building forms of Celtic Ireland before the arrival of the Vikings and early Christianity.

Above right: Meenagahane House

Typical of the 'Thatched Mansions' of the eighteenth century and later, Meenagahane House is a curious link between what some regard as the typical Irish cottage and the simple stone and brick farmhouses of Georgian Ireland. The materials (like thatch and lime-wash) are very much in the vernacular tradition while efforts are made to make its design more contemporary (especially as regards symmetry and proper proportioning, notable in the fenes-tration). This example was demolished around 1978.

Below right: Glenbeigh Towers, Glenbeigh

Sometimes known today as Wynne's Castle, or even Wynne's Folly, Glenbeigh was built over four years from 1867 for one Rowland Winn. The architect was Edward William Godwin, who had it constructed from solid stone to ensure its archaeological correctness. So 'correct' was it that he was sued when it began to leak. A one hundred-foot-tall tower had also been planned but wasn't built. The house was burnt out in 1922 and is today a deceptively medieval-looking ruin.

LIMERICK

Mr Henry David Inglis wrote of Limerick in 1834 that it was 'as lovely a county as the imagination can well picture. In variety, and wooded fertility, it is not surpassed by the most celebrated of the English vales, no one of which can boast as an adjunct to its scenery, so noble a river as the Shannon.' The flat fertile plain of Limerick lies south of the 'noble river', formed of low rolling hills and ringed by mountains. It encompasses the famous 'Golden Vale' of agricultural abundance, which provided its city with much of its wealth.

Limerick, like many Irish towns, assumed a definite outline with the arrival of the Vikings, who established a settlement on an island in the Shannon now known as King's Island. This had previously been the site of a Christian settlement and went on to become the centre of the Kingdom of Thomond. It takes its current moniker, the 'Treaty City', from its war-harried history. It was besieged many times, being a place of strategic importance for crossing the Shannon into the west. Oliver Cromwell's forces took it in 1651 and, following two separate sieges, the city eventually fell to the forces of William III in 1691.

The subsequent treaty granted toleration to Catholicism and full legal rights to Catholics provided they swore an oath to William and his wife Mary. This would later be reneged upon by parliament, who refused to ratify its terms. In exchange the remnants of the Irish army, numbering some 15,000 soldiers, and their families, were allowed go into exile in France, being remembered in history as the 'Wild Geese'.

The relative peace which followed the end of the wars allowed Limerick to prosper and grow. The city expanded, Mr Inglis again writing that 'the new town of Limerick is, unquestionably, superior to any thing out of Dublin. Its principal street, although less picturesque than the chief streets of Cork, would generally be reckoned a finer street. It is straight, regular, and modern-looking; and contains abundance of good private houses and of excellent shops.' Sadly the curse of conflict returned to haunt the city at the opening of the twentieth century. It featured much fighting during the War of Independence, and during the Civil War it suffered eight days of street fighting and the burning of buildings in July of 1922. The county also suffered substantial losses at this time, among them Mountshannon House, once home to the infamous 1st Earl of Clare, John Fitzgibbon.

The opening of Shannon Airport in 1942, just across the river, did much to attract tourism and visitors back to what had become a declining part of the country by the middle of the twentieth century. Although the city and county suffered from much misguided development in the latter half of the century, much remains to be admired. In particular the new town, which was so glowingly described back in 1834, is still well regarded today, as is the old Custom House, the home of the Hunt Museum.

Opposite: Sarsfield Street, Kilmallock

The street, shown in a state of change. An unroofed ruin can be seen in the centre of the picture, towards the end of the street, as can the recently installed telegraph and electricity poles, which oddly enough don't survive today. Nor do so many of the smaller two-storey buildings, replaced with similar structure of less craft and distinction.

Stoic Elegance

Above and right: Mountshannon House, Castleconnell

Mountshannon was once home to John 'Black Jack' Fitzgibbon, 1st Earl of Clare and one time Lord Chancellor of Ireland, who is bitterly remembered as being one of the main protagonists behind the Union between Britain and Ireland in 1800. His house, dating to about 1750, was aggrandised after 1813 for his son, the 2nd Earl, by the architect Lewis Wyatt, who created a stoical, Greek-revival mansion incorporating the earlier building (above). This stoicism extended to the interiors, which were well proportioned but devoid of much ornament, as can be seen from the entrance hall (right). The family eventually fell on hard times, however. In 1888 the palatial contents were sold, and in 1893 the house itself went under the hammer. It was burnt out in 1920 and survives as an overgrown ruin today.

Opposite: Hermitage, Castleconnell

Herimatage was built in 1800 for a banker by the name of Bruce. It had an unusual arrangement of twin pilasters either side of its entrance supporting a small pediment. Between these one entered an equally unusual oval entrance hall. None of this survives today, the house having succumbed to flame in 1920.

Riverside Industry

Opposite: Sarsfield Bridge, Limerick City
This view from Sarsfield (then Wellesley) Bridge shows a riverside crammed with warehouses and factories, a testament to Limerick's prodigious trade connections. None seen here now survive. Industry and export have since been replaced by low-density housing estates and higher density apartment blocks.

Above and right: Old Gaol, Limerick City
This view from Thomond Bridge (above) shows the side of the courthouse on the extreme right, and left of it, Limerick's City Gaol. To the left of that again are Nolan's Cottages. The Gaol had been built in 1789 and was adjacent to the county courthouse. It also backed onto the old county gaol, which still survives. It was quite a dour building, as prisons generally are, but this small door that opened onto St Augustine Place showed some architectural aspiration (right). The gaol and courthouse were demolished, along with the cottages, to make way for new council offices in 1988.

Rural Comforts

Above: Riddlestown Park, Rathkeale

Designed around 1730 by John Rothery, Riddlestown was a grand, imposing block of a house built for the Blennerhassett family, who occupied it until 1904. It was semi-derelict as recently as 10 years ago.

Opposite above: Cahir-Guillamore, Kilmallock

Cahir Guillamore was a substantial late seventeenth-century house, with steep roof and projecting bays at each end. It was the home of the O'Grady family who, in 1831, became Viscounts Guillamore. The Land Commission divided the estate up in 1922, at which time the house was stripped of its fittings and left vacant. It is today a ruin.

Opposite below: Clarina Castle, Clarina

Also known as Elm Park, Clarina Castle was designed by the brother architects James and George Richard Pain around 1828. It was the home of the Massey family, was sold in 1946 and eventually demolished in the 1960s.

Below left and right: Cahirline, Castleconnell

A small, almost square, early nineteenth-century villa with an unusual mix of features. The windows to the front (below right) have gothic-revival hood mouldings over them, and very French-looking shutters either side. To the side is a beautiful gothic cast-iron veranda (below left). The whole composition looked almost Indian.

Going Dutch

Above: Mary Street, Limerick City

The ruins of the old city gaol are seen in the background here, as are a number of Dutch-gabled houses. These houses would have been quite common 'types' built in the late seventeenth and early eighteenth centuries.

Left: Nicholas Street, Limerick City

View up Nicholas Street, looking north. The chancel or east end of St Mary's Cathedral is visible, and still exists. The exchange building, in the centre, was begun in 1673 and was much altered in 1701 and again in 1778. It later became a school, but only its ground-floor arcade now survives. The old house, with its Dutch gable, no longer survives at all.

Above: Cruise's Royal Hotel, O'Connell Street, Limerick City

Cruise's Hotel was something of a landmark on O'Connell Street. It had been established in 1791 and stood where Cruise's Street opens onto O'Connell Street today. It was said to be the oldest hotel in Ireland. It was demolished by developers in 1991 to make way for the new street that today bears its name.

Left: Savoy Theatre, Bedford Row, Limerick City

The Savoy Theatre and Cinema was constructed in 1935 and, when opened, could seat 1,500 people. It closed in 1974 and was demolished in 1988 to make way for a new cinema complex. That too was demolished in 2005.

TIPPERARY

Tipperary is a landscape of contrasts, encompassing as it does ranges of mountains to north and south and sharing the rich pasturelands of the 'Golden Vale' with neighbouring Limerick and Cork. Against this fertile backdrop was played out one of the most mean-spirited and calculated acts of destruction perpetrated on Ireland's heritage, at Shanbally Castle.

Shanbally Castle was built about 1812 for Cornelius O'Callaghan, 1st Viscount Lismore. The castle was situated on a gentle rise of land, sandwiched between the Galtee and the Knockmealdown Mountains of south Tipperary. It was designed by the famous English architect John Nash, architect to the Prince Regent and creator of the Brighton Pavilion. It was the largest of his several projects in Ireland and consisted of a range of battlemented towers of differing shapes and sizes picturesquely dispersed along its irregular form. Complimenting this was an interior richly ornamented with gothic-revival plasterwork. The whole composition sat at the centre of a large walled demesne, which included sizeable swathes of woodland.

The castle made its way through the family generations to the Pole-Carews, cousins of the 2nd and last Viscount Lismore. It was taken over by the military during the 'Emergency' and eventually sold by Major Patrick Pole Carew in 1954 to the Land Commission. It looked as though the Land Commission would sell the house, for which they had no use, and 163 acres to the well-known London theatre critic Edward Charles Sackville-West, 5th Baron Sackville, of Knole House in Kent. He was forced to pull out of the deal however when the Commission refused to stop felling trees on the land which he intended to purchase, and so the house fell into limbo.

With no other buyer forthcoming, it was decided in 1957 that the house should be demolished. This elicited widespread protests. The house had been sold to the government in good order, had only recently been lived in and certainly wasn't 'wholly unoccupied for 40 years' as the government would later state. The protests, and suggestions that it might become home to a school or religious order, fell on deaf ears. It appeared that the Commission had set their mind to it.

The internal fittings were removed, followed by the roof. The battlements were hacked off the towers by hand. The cut stone of the house was dismantled and sold at auction in Limerick. Eventually, making a complete mockery of the Government's claims that it was beyond repair or use, its robust structure was only finally removed from the landscape with the aid of explosives. In March 1960 the local newspaper *The Nationalist* reported: 'A big bang yesterday ended Shanbally Castle, where large quantities of gelignite and cortex shattered the building.' The shattered remains were broken up and used for road building. It cost more to demolish the house than it would have done to keep it. Only one small reminder of it remains, in the form of a ruined two-storey folly, known locally as the tea rooms.

Opposite: West Gate, Irishtown, Clonmel

The West Gate, dating to 1831, still stands today. Much of the pattern and grain of the street has changed; most of the buildings seen on the right of the street have since been demolished and, or, replaced.

Above: Woodrooff House, Clonmel

Woodrooff was a large house built in the middle of the eighteenth century for the Perry family. It was quite a large, plain house to which were later added a pair of impressive wings. These were possibly designed by the architect Davis Ducart and had the unusual distinction of showing up the house they were intended to serve and frame. Each wing formed a courtyard and from the outside they were beautifully enlivened and modulated with niches, blind or blank panels and even a cupola. Sadly the house no longer survives.

Opposite and left: Templemore Abbey, Templemore

Also known as Templemore Priory, the house was built for the Carden family. In the mid eighteenth century a house was built to replace a previous dwelling. It, in turn, was replaced with a new house in 1819 in the gothic style (opposite). This was designed by the architect William Vitruvius Morrison, and was later added to and extended in 1868 when it gained a conservatory (left). The house was occupied during the War of Independence by the Auxiliaries, who used it as a barracks. When they vacated it in 1921, it was burnt out by the IRA to prevent it being used as such again and was later demolished.

Above left: Ballinaclough House, Nenagh

A charming, average-sized house with arched, round-headed windows of different types. Ballinaclough was representative of the late Victorian picturesque, set in mature grounds and itself enveloped in vegetation.

Below left: Kilboy House, Nenagh

Kilboy was a supremely impressive house for its size, designed by the amateur architect William Leeson around 1780. The house was home to the Prittie family, later Lords Dunalley. Burnt out in 1922, it was rebuilt without its top, attic floor. That rebuilding was demolished in the mid 1950s and replaced with a smaller house on top of the original raised basement.

Below right: The Rock, Cashel

A view of the famous Rock of Cashel shows a line of small, vernacular houses lining the road leading to it. The small square windows and half doors are typical of their time and would once have been seen on so many small homes in Ireland. They no longer survive.

Opposite: West Gate, Carrick-on-Suir

An early eighteenth-century house full of character, thanks in part to its covering of slate. Particularly delightful were the small triangular patterns between the arches of each window. Although the building survives, its slate has been stripped off and its original windows replaced. Almost all its charm and character has gone with them.

Municipal Delights

Right: Charter School, Cashel

The Charter school was built around 1751 and has been linked to the architect Richard Castle. It was a rather solid building that was gently handled by whoever designed it. It no longer survives.

Below: Military Barracks, The Square, Fethard

The military barracks was actually once a grand house, built by one Thomas Barton on the site of the house of Sir John Everard, which he had demolished in 1752. It was taken over as a temporary barracks in 1797, and remained as one thereafter. It was taken over by anti-Treaty forces in 1922 and torched by them soon after to prevent it being occupied by the forces of the Free State.

Opposite above: Friar Street, Cashel

A view, again, towards the famous Rock. The street is little seen from this view, but has ceded some of its homely charm to modern shopfronts and paint colours.

Below: Main Guard, Clonmel

This image shows the Main Guard before its restoration in 2000. Although the building has been lovingly restored to its original form it is curious to see it here, divided up into three storeys rather than its original two, with shops on the ground floor. It is a perfect illustration of the constant layering of history.

Nash's Gothic-Revival Masterpiece

All: Shanbally Castle, Clogheen

Shanbally was the largest of the several castles constructed to the designs of John Nash, architect to the Prince Regent (later King George IV), in Ireland. It was built of silver-grey ashlar and was the epitome of the chivalric, fairytale castle of the imagination. Entry was to a relatively low hall, lit from above and decorated with plaster fan-vaulting, that led to a soaring imperial staircase (opposite left). The ceiling of the staircase itself was even more impressive (above right). Along the garden front (above left) were arranged a series of reception rooms including a dining room in the octagonal tower on the right, a drawing room in the circular room on the left and a library in the middle, the interior of which was again decorated with delicate creamy plasterwork (above right). The house also had 20 bedrooms. It was a well-built pleasure palace set in its own mature, landscaped grounds that was destroyed by malice and indifference in 1957.

God, in the Details

Above: Cathedral of the Assumption, Cathedral Street, Thurles
The Cathedral at Thurles was begun in 1861 to the design of J.J. McCarthy with the interior completed by George Ashlin. That interior, illustrated here, was an elaborate affair. Although no major demolition was initiated following on from Vatican II, much of the ornament here has been painted over or removed.

Left: O'Connell Street, Clonmel
A fantastically elaborate gothic-revival door to the right of, and forming part of, a larger shop front. This illustrates the levels of detail that were lavished on such commercial constructions, being intended to give a good impression of the store and its proprietor. Sadly, they are too often the first things dispensed with by new owners.

Opposite above: Market House, Main Street, Roscrea
Once situated at the junction of Main Street and Castle Street, right in the middle of the road, the market house would have been the focal point of the regular markets and fairs that took place in this part of the town. Likely dating from the early nineteenth century, it no longer survives.

Below: William O'Brien Arcade, Dillon Street, 'New' Tipperary

Constructed by tenants following a dispute with their landlord and the withholding of their rents to him, the arcade was a part of a 'new' town constructed on land the landlord had no control over.

The arcade didn't last long. Agreement was reached between the landlord, Smith-Barry, and the tenant and the arcade was demolished in 1892, just a few years after it had been constructed.

WATERFORD

The rivers of the Suir, the Nore and the Barrow, 'the three sisters', between them drain a large portion of the rich pastureland in the southeast corner of Ireland. All three come together in the same bay at the 'confluence of the three waters' and from there enter the Atlantic. Just upriver of this bay, sitting between the banks of the Suir and John's river, is sandwiched the ancient city of Waterford. Such a setting, within the naturally formed aquatic fissures of the coastline, correctly suggests the presence of the Vikings and indeed Waterford was laid out in the classic mould of the Viking town.

It was established by the marauding, sea-trading Scandinavians in 853AD. Reginald's Tower, its oldest landmark, takes its name from the Viking King of the city, Ragnall, who was imprisoned there after the city's capture by the Normans. It is reputed to be the oldest structure built with mortar in Ireland. The Normans rebuilt the city's defences and throughout the middles ages Waterford was Ireland's second city after Dublin. It was here that Henry II landed in 1171, when he came to Ireland to assert his authority over his own conquering knights as well as the native Irish lords and kings.

The city continued as an important port, given its proximity to Britain and Europe, and the eighteenth century saw a time of great expansion. At the beginning of the century this growth saw the old city wall, which had protected the citizens from attack from the river, demolished. The rubble was used to construct a new quay on the river's edge. This became the hub of Waterford's trade. The quay itself was a mile long, one of the largest of its time, and it remains today one of the grandest to be seen anywhere. This was the place where ships were docked and unloaded and from which they were loaded up again with Irish produce, such as bacon, butter and corn, and sent around the world.

The boom continued into the nineteenth century, when shipbuilding became an important activity, seen in the establishment of dockyards like White's and the Neptune shipyard. Glass, which had been made in the city as far back as 1783, was another industry that grew rapidly at this time, and the city is still famous for its cut crystal today.

Such a hub of commerce would have been home to a riot of different shops, emporiums and stores, located on the quays and on the streets leading to them. These are generally the least resilient element of the built fabric of a city and have survived less well. Many have been painted over or been swapped for newer, more 'modern' designs. In the saddest cases their whole building has disappeared. But much remains in this ancient city, and it well rewards a visit today.

Opposite: Waterford City
General View of Waterford City from the north. Stretching across from right to left is its famous mile-long quay and crossing the river is the old wooden trestle bridge known locally as 'Timbertoes', replaced between 1910 and 1913 with Redmond Bridge.

Harbourside Commerce

Opposite above: Mary Street, Waterford City

A view down Mary Street, once a hive of industrial and commercial activity, as witnessed by the two chimney stacks which are visible over the rooftops. Strangman's Brewery was established here in 1792. Most of the street has since been replaced with modern apartment blocks.

Opposite below left and right: Broad Street, Waterford City

Once the main commercial street in Waterford, Broad Street boasted shops like J. Morgan's Butchers (left) and a Home and Colonial Store (right). Both had shop fronts were of simple, yet elegant, design. Neither survives.

Above: The Mall, Waterford City

Here we see the north-east end of the Mall, with Reginald's Tower on the right and two ranges of Georgian buildings opposite. These were home to two well-known hotels: the Adelphi Hotel occupied most of the range on the left and the Imperial Hotel most of that on the right. The Imperial was demolished in the 1960s and the Adelphi in the 1970s. Both sites are today occupied by the Tower Hotel, a rather oversized, lifeless block.

Above: Harbour, Dunmore East

Dunmore was an important fishing port, as can be readily seen by the plethora of boats in the water. The pier on the right, was built in the early nineteenth century, but of more interest is the range of natural rock on the left. In particular the small gothic bridge linking the two outcrops of rock shows a sensitivity and practicality not much seen today.

Opposite below: Malcomson's Cotton Factory, Portlaw

This vast industrial complex has a truly chequered history. It was founded by the Malcomson family in 1826 and consisted of a large six storey, 15 bay mill that was added to and altered over the years. Shown here are the two large water wheels that would have powered the original mill. The complex closed in 1904 and was reopened after much renovation in 1945 as a tannery. The tannery lasted until 1985. The site is now derelict.

Below: Flynn & Young Fishmongers, Conduit Lane, Waterford City

The fishmongers was strategically located near the quay to avail itself of the freshest stocks of seafood. The utilitarian design, glazed tiles and stone floor would have allowed for easy washing. Most similar interiors have given way to health and safety concerns today.

Above: Greyfriars, Waterford City

Greyfriars was established by the Franciscans in 1240 and continued as a religious institution until 1540. The city grew up around it and here can be seen some of the old houses, possibly of the early eighteenth century, that backed onto it. Also of interest is the hoarding around them, used much like today's are, for advertising. These houses were cleared away in the 1860s to make way for the street now known as 'Greyfriars'.

Religious Influence

Above: Cathedral of the Most Holy Trinity, Barronstrand Street, Waterford City

Ireland's oldest Roman Catholic cathedral was designed by the architect John Roberts in 1793, and extended and altered several times after that. Of interest here are the beautiful painted 'grotesques' on the ceiling. They have not survived the cathedral's impressive history, possibly removed around the time of Vatican II.

Right: Grantstown House, Earlscourt, Waterford

An early nineteenth-century house which was once the home to the Bishop Foy School. It has a particularly pretty bowed projection to its garden side, shown here. The form of the building survives, converted into apartments in the 1990s, and it is today nestled within a modern housing estate.

Victorian Curiosities

Above: Roseville, Lismore

A mid nineteenth-century Victorian villa which, with Glenville (opposite) give a good flavour of the variety of tastes at the time. Roseville was a large gothic house, made to appear more like a cottage with its heavy gothic detailing, such as its bargeboards and windows. Of great curiosity is the overblown gothic conservatory seen on the right. With so much detail and material gone into the structure it's unlikely that it allowed in much more light than the house itself.

Above and below: Glenville, Waterford

Glenville was a mid nineteenth-century house, or villa, in a mildly Italianate style, built for the Hassard family. To the left of the entrance front, with its porch, can be seen a greenhouse or conservatory with a gothic-pointed frame (top). The interior was a similar Victorian mix of the eclectic, the entrance hall being a de-facto trophy room, adorned with the heads and skins of many beasts hunted while on holiday. The house was sold in 1957 and, following a fire, was soon after demolished.

Opposite: Old House, off Arundel Square, Waterford City
The exact location of this house is unknown, but it was a great hybrid of different eras. The way the upper floors overhang the ground floor is almost medieval in form, while the windows are of the early eighteenth century. Likely it was a building that was adapted and changed over time. Would that it would have done so to the present day.

Left: Mary Mason School, Lady Lane, Waterford City
The Girl's Blue School was founded in 1740 on Lady Lane by one Mary Mason and the building it occupied later came to be known as the Mary Mason School. It was an early eighteenth-century house, with a high pediment. It was demolished in 1965.

Below: Waterford Hounds, Waterford City
It is easy to forget that, although distinctly separate, there was not the division between town and country in the past as there is today. This may partially be due to the relative size of towns and cities in the past and the closer proximity of the countryside, but also to the fact that local produce was sold locally. Seen here is the Waterford Hunt, gathered in the city in 1903, before they take to the countryside for the chase, such was the closeness of open fields back then.

Age-Old Traditions

CONNAUGHT

GALWAY

The most prominent and famous of all the Connaught counties, this was this place that Oliver Cromwell had in mind when he uttered his famous ultimatum 'To Hell or to Connaught.' Hedges give way to stone walls, pasture to bogland, and rolling hills to majestic mountains. The landscape is one of rugged beauty, which despite its inhospitable nature has drawn visitors for centuries.

The county takes its name from the city at its heart. Galway has long been the capital of Connaught, developing as an important trading port with Europe from the earliest times. The most prominent resulting influence is Spanish, which was remarked on by many visitors. One, M.M. Shoemaker, writing in 1908, recalled that 'Spanish traits and features intermingled with the Celtic, and many of its ancient houses hold the touch of the South in their lines.' During the Middle Ages 14 merchant families, remembered today as the 'Tribes of Galway', dominated the town, and it was largely under their control that trade thrived and it became the main Irish port trading with the continent.

The Great Famine of the 1840s hit Galway hard, and huge numbers emigrated or died. The landscape was unwelcoming enough to those of little means, and in some ways Galway never recovered. What the famine destroyed, railways and tourism went some way towards remedying, bringing new sources of employment and much-needed capital into the county. Many hotels sprang up to cater to the visitors' needs, generally next to railway stations and sponsored by the railway companies themselves. Such was the attraction of Galway that an Indian Maharaja, His Highness Kumar Shri Ranjitsinhji, purchased Ballynahinch Castle and its 30,000 acres there in 1924. He is remembered locally today as 'Ranji'.

Ballynahinch Castle survives today as an hotel, but not so Eyrecourt (opposite, also p. 248), an important and impressive house which was allowed to fall into a state of decay. The building was stripped of its famous staircase, which was bought by William Randolph Hearst for Hearst Castle, California. The staircase later made its way to the Detroit Institute of Arts, where reputedly it still languishes in its packing crates. It would be better served being on display, if not in the United States, them maybe in Ireland?

Ardfry is an interesting case for its truly odd later demise. Having been allowed to fall into dereliction it was used as a movie set for the film *The Mackintosh Man*, starring Paul Newman and released in 1973. For this the house was reroofed and had new windows installed, only to be intentionally burnt for one of the film's scenes. What tentatively survived of the original features before this was totally lost and the house, having experienced a brief moment of much-needed attention, was left in a far worse state of deterioration. It still survives as a picturesque ruin today, though it may be better appreciated in the film.

Opposite: Eyrecourt Castle, Eyrecourt
Members of the local hunt posing in front of the grand entrance door to Eyrecourt. To describe it as fantastical doesn't do it justice.

Practical Innovations

Above left: T. Waters and M. Hayes, Gort

The charming image, possibly of a house that once stood on the Market Square in Gort, epitomises the country town. A large house, with simple details such as the tripartite first floor window and the elegant cut-stone doorway below, would once have been a large, impressive family home. It was likely at a later time that the shops were added, but they sit quietly in the façade, sharing its quiet understatement.

Above right: Ordnance Survey Trigonometric Station, Galway

This is a curious image of one of the many stations, sometimes also called Triangulation Pillars, that were erected across the island for drafting and compiling the Ordnance Survey Maps.

Opposite above: Salmon Weir, Galway City

Just outside the city, this clever yet makeshift arrangement of wooden traps and stone piers allowed for the catching of wild salmon on the River Corrib.

Opposite below: Fishmarket, Galway City

This small collection of houses, strategically gathered around a small open square, would have witnessed the almost-daily landing of fish from boats returning from sea. Very little of the square remains, most of the houses are gone, as is the bridge, though the Spanish Arch, to the right, survives.

Unexpected Beauty

All above: Lisreaghan House, Lawrencetown

Lisreaghan (sometimes known as Bellevue) was one of those great Irish architectural quirks, possessing all or more of the requisite elements of greatness, but arranged in the most unusual, but pleasing, way. The house was built in the eighteenth century for one Walter Lawrence, and was likely an extension of an existing house given its length. Its portico, though grand, was rather lost in the length of the façade. The interiors were lavish, the Aurora Hall (above left) having a fine set of murals and the Library (above right) a robust, unusual coved ceiling. Nothing now remains of the house, which was demolished in the 1920s.

Above: Glasshouses, Kylemore Abbey

A vast range of glasshouses at Kylemore Abbey, built alongside the house, or Abbey, from 1867 to 1871 by the architect James Franklin Fuller. There were over twenty individual glasshouses, including a banana house that ran to sixty feet in length. The gardens ran wild after the Duke of Manchester bought the estate in 1909, during which time most of the glasshouses deteriorated. It was bought by an order of Benedictine nuns from Ypres, Belgium, following the First World War. Some, but not all, of the glasshouses have since been restored.

Right: Bridge, Glen Inagh, Connemara

In the wild, exposed landscape for which Galway is famous, there was little material available from which to construct necessary infrastructure. This modest bridge, of local stone, shows off the resourcefulness of the local population in both its material and modesty.

Above: Castle Daly, Loughrea

Castle Daly, as the name might imply, was the home of the Daly family, who purchased a house here in 1829. The original house was constructed in the early eighteenth century, incorporating an earlier tower house, and was 'castellated' in the nineteenth century by its new Daly owners. Part of the wall, shown here, survives today as a picturesque ruin.

Above: Monivea Castle, Athenry

A house built for one Patrick Ffrench between 1713 and 1715 and consisting of two ranges of accommodation extending from an earlier tower house, forming an 'L'. It was added to and altered in the nineteenth century and was left by Kathleen Ffrench to the Irish state to provide a home for Irish artists. Her request was ignored and all except the old tower was demolished.

Both above: Eyrecourt Castle, Eyrecourt

The estate at Eyrecourt came into the possession of Colonel John Eyre in 1662, following which he constructed the building known as Eyrecourt Castle. It was one of the earliest undefended houses to be built in the country and as such was an important milestone in Irish architectural history. Its chief glory was its bucolically carved staircase consisting of two flights rising from the hall to a half landing, from which a third, central, flight reached the first floor. The family fell on hard times and by the 1920s the house had been abandoned. It was stripped of its main fittings and is today an overgrown ruin, though nothing is ever beyond saving.

Home as Castle

Left: Ardfry, Oranmore

A large, long house built about 1770 for the Blake family, later Lords Wallscourt. It was remodelled in 1826, at which time it may have gained its gothic features and the small domes atop the pavilion-like ends of the house. In the early twentieth century the lead was stripped from the roof and sold to pay gambling debts. It declined only to suffer the indignity of being reroofed and reglazed for a film, in which it was subsequently set on fire.

Below: Farmstead, Killary Harbour

A group of buildings tightly grouped together in a linear fashion along the mountainside, overlooking the famous coastal inlet. The arrangement is reflective of the terrain, spread out in a long line to keep everything on a roughly similar level. The materials, from stone and thatch to rendered walls and slate, suggest continuous development over the years, as circumstances improved for the owner.

Getting Around

Left: Stables, Eyrecourt Castle, Eyrecourt

A grand block of stables constructed to serve the 'Castle' described on the previous pages. The central section, below the steep pediment, would have housed carriages behind its large doors, with stalls for horses hidden behind the modest doors either side. In the age of the motor, horses were replaced with cars, which fit snugly into the place of the old carriages.

Below left: Browne's Grove, Ballyconneely

Lying on a peninsula jutting out into the Atlantic, slate was probably a clever choice of cladding for this small, early nineteenth-century house that may have incorporated an earlier house of about 1770. It was built by Thomas Browne who bought the estate of Joycegrove in the 1850s and then renamed it after his own family. As well as its textured covering, it had an unusual protruding central bay, which was curved at its corners.

Below right: Transport Car, Galway

The sightseeing bus and general mode of public transport of its day, these horse-drawn cars provided the most reliable way of moving from town to town in the west of Ireland up until the arrival of the motor car.

LEITRIM

This part of the world has always been a slightly stark and untamed place. The county is long and thin, famously having the shortest coastline of any in Ireland, and is effectively split in two by the large expanse of Lough Allen. To the north-west the land is rugged and mountainous, to the south-west more gentle – dappled with lakes and wetlands.

In ancient times Leitrim was part of the kingdom of Breffni, and it was from here that Ireland's 'Helen of Troy' – Dervorgilla, wife of the King – was abducted by the king of Leinster, Dermot Mac Murrough. War between the two kings, understandably, followed. Dermot lost and was banished. He made his way to the court of Henry II and there solicited help to regain his kingdom. The help came in the form of Henry's barons, famous among them being Richard de Clare, Earl of Pembroke, better known as 'Strongbow'. Strongbow arrived in Ireland near Waterford in 1169, helped Dermot regain his throne, married his daughter, and positioned himself to be the next king of Leinster. To counter this, Henry II himself made his way to Ireland and forced Strongbow, as well as the native Gaelic kings, to pledge their loyalty to him. Kings of England were thereafter also known as Lords of Ireland.

The county has always been sparsely populated, and largely agricultural or wild. It is well remembered that the epitome of the heartless landlord of modern cliché was William Sydney Clements, the infamous 3rd Earl of Leitrim. Famously hard on his tenants and enthusiastic to evict them, he was assassinated, having survived several previous attempts, in 1878. No one was ever apprehended in connection with it. His magnificent house, Lough Rynn, still stands today.

The relative size of the population is reflected, ripple-like, in the relative quantity of its building stock, in what has been lost of it, and consequently, what images we have of it before it was lost. During the Famine the county was decimated, its already-small population diminishing by almost a third. Emigration continued after the Famine meaning that to this day Leitrim is Ireland's least populated county. Many of its small vernacular homes, like the one on page 256, simply would have melted away once the family had been evicted or left, with no one left to keep them in good repair.

One of the images shows the aftermath of the 'Cloudburst', a freak weather event that wrecked havoc on the county in the early 1930s. The sky grew black and produced a massive rainstorm resulting in flash floods. The roaring sound of this could be heard for miles. Many houses were destroyed 'by the breaking in of the flood'. Livestock was swept away, as was the hay which was being made at the time, 'and was to be seen sailing in the lakes' days after.

Opposite: Main Street, Leitrim
The Main Street, Leitrim, dotted as so many small towns once were with various shops and stalls but, strikingly, devoid of the Dickensian filth we associate in our minds with such places. In fact it would make many of today's towns look untidy!

Left: Train Wagon Shop, Ballinamore

Ballinamore was once an important stop on the Cavan Leitrim railway line, which opened in 1883. It was also the location for the repair shops and workshops where the work of maintaining the trains was carried out. One such shop is seen here, a hybrid of Victorian iron trusses and glazed roofing combined with walls of local materials. The train line was closed in 1959, the land subsequently sold off and many of the associated buildings, such as the wagon repair shop, demolished.

Above: St Patrick's Church, Mohill

St Patrick's is a peculiarity in that it was designed by a member of the clergy, one Canon Donohue, and built in 1886, reputedly from voluntary labour solicited by the Canon from the local congregation. Its modest appearance was enhanced by the addition of a tower in 1936. Its interior would have been vividly enlivened by painting and decoration on the various wall surfaces. This was all removed or painted over during renovations in the 1960s, which have left the building feeling somewhat stark.

Splendid Isolation

Above right: Castle Gate, Mohill

The gate to Mohill Castle was a simple structure of local materials. The distance from the large metropolitan centres meant that pretentions didn't have to be too assertive. Like so many other relatively isolated estates, the supporting infrastructure would have been quite plain, in the vein of the vernacular. Unlike the gate and gatehouse seen here, these smaller, more manageable buildings tended to outlast the larger houses and castles that they once served.

Below right: Bridge, Glencar

The landscape in this part of the world, although beautiful, is unforgiving. The magnificent scenery belies the fact that nature provides very little with which to work. Stone is the only resource, and it would have been used for all structural endeavours. This bridge is typical of the many that would have been fashioned, largely without the help of architects, all across the country. Their simple, timeless design makes them tricky to date. Many have fallen foul of the structural necessity required by modern traffic.

Opposite above: Ruined Homestead, Leitrim

These houses, ruined during a freak weather event known locally as the 'Cloudburst' that caused flash floods in the early 1930s, provide an interesting cross-section of the typical vernacular house. Simple rubble walls, rendered without and wallpapered within, all kept dry under a simple roof of thatch. The glimpse of the interior here is particularly interesting, showing a room much more homely than popular stereotype would have us imagine.

Opposite below: Shop, Leitrim

This small shop is really just a home, in which, over the years, a small business has developed. The only clue from the outside of its commercial aspect is the enlarged window with goods displayed against the glass. Very few instances of such early 'shops' survive, but they would have been the seed from which the modern equivalent developed.

Genteel Comfort

Left: Drumhierny Lodge, Leitrim

Drumhierny was a relatively impressive large house, plain but simple, with a pediment in its centre breaking forward from the elevation lending it some dynamism. It was home to a branch of the La Touche family who sold it in 1912. Later it was occupied by the O'Raghallaighs. Today it is a ruin.

Right: Jamestown House, Drumsna

Jamestown was home to the O'Beirne family, the original house having been built about 1780. The image here shows it after an extensive remodelling in the nineteenth century, when it was reroofed and acquired the curious semi-circular lunettes below its new roofing. It was significantly remodelled again in the 1930s, losing much of its Georgian/Victorian hybrid character.

Below: Kinlough House, Kinlough

Kinlough House was an early nineteenth-century home of some style and pretention built by one Robert Johnston. The ground-floor windows are set within arched recesses and the portico is sturdy yet decorative. It is today much more ruinous than it appears here.

MAYO

The name 'Mayo' comes from the Gaelic meaning 'plain of yew trees', yet to the popular imagination the county is devoid of trees, austere and bleak in its Irish-alpine beauty. The south affords better land for pasture, but northward the landscape assumes the form described above, patterned with the browns of bogland and the greys, ranging in tone from green to pink, of the bare mountain escarpments.

Such a landscape would appear inhospitable, and yet Henry Spencer Wilkinson, writing in 'The Eve of Home Rule: Impressions of Ireland' in 1886, is surprised by what he discovers on travelling through the county. 'These Irish wilds differ from the English ones' he writes. 'Here they are covered with habitations, and are the home of a large population. As far as we can see … we find the hillside sprinkled with cottages, and the ground divided by low stone and turf fences into innumerable fields.' These fields had 'been won from the bog by years of infinite labour… But wherever such a field is neglected for a while the bog reclaims its rights.'

This portrait, of a life eked out in constant conflict with the forces of nature and her meagre provisions, was reflected in the architecture of the poorer dwellings. In the most unfortunate of situations these consisted of little more than the upturned sods of the ground underfoot, formed into a sort of wall or bank, upon which rested a makeshift roof of more sod, or foliage. For all of their inhospitable presence, they reflected an ingenuity and resourcefulness, which is to be much admired and respected.

In the equally harsh, but less muddy surrounds of the mountainside, a more robust home could be made of local stone, its roof tied down to its walls in the hope that such pretence to permanence would not offend the elements. The landscape is littered today with the surviving mounds of stone which once formed the walls of these abandoned homes, a stark reminder of the hardship such an existence entailed.

The structures of the towns and of the wealthier landowners provide an extreme contrast to these basic constructions. Those who could afford it built larger and more robustly, but even their efforts did not always ensure survival. Decline in population and political unrest often meant a paralleled decline in personal fortunes, and so many of those houses which once stood so awkwardly in contrast to their primitive neighbours have joined them as ruined piles of stone, disappearing back into the bogland of County Mayo.

Opposite: Clare Island
Castle and cottage, permanence and defence, alongside unaggressive domesticity. This image contrasts two of the main forms buildings took in earlier times.

Vernacular Ingenuity

These images illustrate the ingenuity and resourcefulness of the vernacular builder. Materials were sourced from as near as possible and when the obvious, durable choice of stone was not to hand, clay and the soil were used.

The image top left shows rolls of sods cut from the surface of the ground and rolled up, ready to be used for covering a roof in the absence of thatch.

Immediately below it is a clever solution to the problem of 'building' a structure, which has instead been partially excavated and then roofed. This particular structure, at Bellacorrick, was used for sheltering livestock.

The third image down shows a more obvious use of the earth. This dwelling at Tooraree consisted of low walls, which could just about be described as 'built', though they come very close to almost being just piled up mounds of earth. Resting on top of these footings is a roof of vegetation. This would have been the type of home that many of the poorer, landless labourers built for themselves and their families at the side of the road.

The house in the picture at the bottom of the page shows a much more permanent structure of stone and thatch. It would originally have been half the size shown here, ending at the chimney in the middle of the roof, but has later been extended by adding onto the end of the house.

Opposite we can see the end of a similar house at Dooagh. The crossover of skills from agriculture to building is nicely pointed up by the hay rick next to the building, which would have been similarly thatched to keep the rain off. The stepped gable of the house is curious. It is usually associated with Scotland and leads us to wonder whether it was intentional or just easier than working the stone to form a smooth pitch.

Palatial Surprise

Left: Killala Castle, Killala

The castle at Killala was also known as the Bishop's palace as it was the residence of the Protestant Archbishop of Killala and Achonry. Parts of the building were said to date back to the sixteenth century, though as can be seen here it was much remodelled and extended at a later date. It was occupied by the troops of General Humbert during the French landing of 1798 and was damaged during the 'Big Wind' of 1839. It was demolished in the 1950s.

Above left and right: Hollymount House, Hollymount

Hollymount was an early eighteenth-century house constructed for the Archbishop of Tuam, John Vesey. It passed, through marriage, to the Lindsey family who, around 1834, commissioned the architect George Papworth to re-front it in the heavily articulated manner seen here (above left). It continued to be occupied up until 1922 when, although not a casualty of the war at the time, it was vacated. By the 1940s it was derelict and it is today a ruin. The gate piers (above right), which give a clue as to the crispness and delicacy of the original house, were later moved and re-erected in Kinsale, Co. Cork.

Above: Deverell's Shop, Main Street, Newport

This small local shop is unusual in that it is formed largely from the wall of the building and not from a carved wooden front applied to it. The piers between the windows and doors are decorated with an almost abstract, simple line design, reminiscent of the work of the British architect John Soane. As in so many cases, the building survives but the shop elements have been eradicated.

Right: O'Rattigan's Bar, Castlebar

A delightful shop front, simple and utilitarian. It might be thought an odd design for a pub, but it was quite common that pub and grocery store would be located behind the same front door, especially in smaller towns and villages. It is seldom the case now.

Railway Prosperity

Above: Railway Station, Newport

Newport train station was opened in 1894, following several years' construction on the tunnel you see in the photograph and a large seven-arched viaduct that bridged a river valley in the opposite direction. It was part of an initiative to bring the benefits of the railways to disadvantaged parts of the country. Most likely due to some idea of 'rationalizing' the rail network, Newport station was closed in 1937.

ROSCOMMON

For a relatively under-populated county Roscommon has produced, and lost, some fine examples of the architectural craft. Indeed, only two of its eighteenth-century 'big houses', Strokestown Park and the King House, survive today. Among the losses are a surprising number of large Palladian mansions, including the 'palace' built for the Bishop of Elphin in the 1740s (p. 277) and the slightly earlier French Park designed by Richard Castle about 1729 (p. 277). Both had large central blocks linked by curved sweeps or arms to smaller wings and both are sadly now lost.

Of a similar type was Mantua House, also linked with Richard Castle and constructed some time around 1747 (p. 278). It was built for Oliver Grace, who had married the heiress to the Mantua estate and expressed his joy at such a marriage, as well as the wealth it brought him, through the house he built there. It sat at the centre of a large estate, framed by wings on either side, and was later adorned with elaborate gardens including terraces and a fishpond. In the nineteenth century the house was shorn of its adjoining wings and sweeps, which were demolished. The central block remained but was later abandoned and is now a ruin. A visit to Mantua in 1908 gives an interesting insight to Irish superstitions and is provided by M.M Shoemaker in his 'Wanderings in Ireland'. He described Mantua as 'a cheery, pleasant abiding-place ... [that]... smiles at the passer-by like a saintly old lady. It is said that the fairies abided once under its doorstep and when some few years ago a vestibule

was added an old woman appeared and kneeling down cursed the workmen for disturbing them. But the little spirits do not seem to have minded it much and the inhabitants of the "House in the Bog" live on in peace. My night's slumber under its roof was undisturbed and dreamless.' One wonders how the fairies might feel today; the ruins of the house are choked with vegetation as it is slowly reclaimed by nature.

Standing out among such rarefied architectural company was the most notable house in the county, Rockingham, designed by John Nash and built in 1810. It lost much of its original élan following alterations, which included the addition of an extra floor later in the century. This replaced the large dome that had been the centrepiece of the composition. Although aesthetically reduced by these alterations, it still created an impressive vista when viewed across Lough Key, above which it stood (pp. 240–41, 279). It was gutted by an accidental fire in 1957 and the remains of the house were later demolished. The fantastic setting of this once great house is now open to the public in the form of Lough Key Forest Park.

Opposite: Old Gaol, Roscommon
Shown here when used as a Market House, it survives today, though now as a shopping centre and apartments.

Atmospheric Interiors

Below left: Old Gaol, The Square, Roscommon

This impressive and intimidating building was constructed by the local landlord, the Earl of Essex, around 1740 and is locally said to have been designed by the architect Richard Castle, who worked nearby. It served a variety of functions over the years, becoming a lunatic asylum, later a market house and then a private house. This image shows part of the atmospheric interior that was swept away when, for whatever reason, it was allowed be converted into a shopping centre in the 1980s. It remains as such today.

Below right: The King House, Boyle

This atmospheric interior belongs to King House, built for Sir Henry King in the early eighteenth century, possibly in the 1720s. It has the unusual feature of each floor being composed of brick vaults, possibly a precaution against fire. The Kings later became Earls of Kingston and moved to Rockingham House, at which point they sold King House to the government in 1795 and it became a barracks. It continued as such until the middle of the twentieth century, at which point it fell into private ownership and then into a state of considerable decay. It was on the brink of being demolished when Roscommon County Council bought it in 1987 and began to restore it. This picture gives some idea of its original condition. Although much better restored, one can't help but think some of the atmosphere disappeared at that time too.

Opposite: Gateway, Mote Park, Ballymurray

A supremely impressive entrance gate in the form of a triumphal arch, built in the late eighteenth or early nineteenth century. It has been tentatively linked to the architect James Gandon. It survives today, much as it appears here, but its presence has been lost to an assortment of agricultural buildings which encumber it.

Aristocratic Parkland

Above: Mote Park, Ballymurray

Mote was a large, plain house, home to the Crofton family, and was built between 1777 and 1787. It is shown here as it was rebuilt following a fire in 1880. Some of the changes made in the rebuilding include the extension of the main block, just hidden behind the tree on the left, and the enclosing of the portico. These alterations served to make it quite oppressive, almost literally weighing down the original house. It was sold in the 1950s and demolished thereafter.

Right: Corregard House, Boyle

Sometimes also called Corrigard, this handsome little house was home to the Peyton family. Here we see it framed by trees that line the approach to it, a reminder of how integral landscape was to larger houses. In the cases where such buildings are lucky enough to survive, it is much less likely that the setting of their grounds do.

Pastoral Grandeur

Above: Mount Talbot, Athleague

Mount Talbot was a peculiar house. It began life, in 1749, as a Palladian mansion linked by curved walls to two wings. These wings were set at forty-five degree angles to the main house. Around 1820 its owners, the Talbot family, remodelled the main block as a gothic-revival castle, the central rear projection of which can be seen here. The wings however remained classical. It was burnt out in 1922 and later broken up by the Land Commission.

Opposite above: French Park, Frenchpark

A large, impressive redbrick mansion built by John French in about 1729, with Richard Castle as his architect. The house was sold in 1953 by the 7th Lord Freyne (the title that the French family had acquired). Its owners, the Land Commission, unroofed the house and stripped it of its interior fittings. The ruins were eventually demolished in the 1970s.

Opposite middle: Bishop's Palace, Elphin

The home of a bishop is always styled a 'palace'. This palace was built between 1747 and 1749 for Edward Synge, the Bishop of Elphin. It was a handsome building, Palladian in composition with wings linked to the main house by curved sweeps. It was designed by one Michael Wills, evidently an accomplished if unknown architect, and survived until an accidental fire destroyed it in 1911. It was subsequently demolished.

Opposite below: Charlestown House, Clogher

A pleasant and unassuming gentleman's house of the late Georgian period situated overlooking the river Shannon. The house no longer survives.

Above and left: Mantua House, Castlerea

Mantua was constructed around 1747 to the designs of the architect Richard Castle for one Oliver Grace. It is shown here, shorn of its wings. They would originally have been of two storeys high and three bays wide, with a Venetian window occupying the central bay and a recessed roundel above. They, and their connecting arms, were demolished in the nineteenth century, leaving the house as it appeared above. Its interiors were finely decorated, a small glimpse of which is gained through the remains of the plasterwork and woodwork of the stair hall, left. The house is today an overgrown ruin.

Western Opulence

All: Rockingham House, Boyle

Rockingham was once the finest house in the county. It had been designed by John Nash and built in 1810 for General Robert King. Later, in 1822, an extra floor was added to the house, which took much of its elegance away. It was rebuilt following a fire in 1863, but not after a second one in 1957. It contained some wonderful interiors, such as the top-lit hall (below, centre).

It stood at the centre of a magnificent estate, the house itself perched high above Lough Key. Life was all about leisure back then, dogs were kept for hunting (below right) and gardens laid out for relaxing walks. The orangery, right, was added in the late nineteenth century. Following the second fire it was sold to the Land Commission who demolished the house and opened the estate as a Forest Park to the public.

Above and below left: Longford House, Beltra

Longford House was built as a home for the Crofton family in 1782. Originally it was intended to have two wings, linked to the house with arms, but only one of these ever materialised. It has had the misfortune of suffering several major fires over its history. The first of these was about 1816, following which the main house was vacated and the adjoining wing fitted up as a residence. It in turn was struck by fire in 1840 and 1916. The main house today is a ruin, having previously been fitted up as a store.

Within the grounds is an interesting chimneypiece from Mote Park in nearby Roscommon (pp. 273-74). It is inscribed 'George Crofton 1632 Elizabeth Crofton' and possibly celebrates their marriage in that year (below left).

Opposite and below right: Cloonamahon House, Collooney

Cloonamahon was begun in 1856 to the designs of one Mr Montgomery for Captain T.J. Meredith. It was a piece of exaggerated Victorian revivalism, and was reputedly cursed. The Captain died before it was completed and the house proceeded to be plagued with water seeping in through the walls. It was sold in the early twentieth century and was used by the Passionist Fathers, a religious organisation. It was eventually demolished in 1976 and the site is today home to a health facility.

The chimneypiece gives some insight into the interiors, which appear to have been just as exuberant as the exterior.

The County Town

Below: Grattan Street, Sligo Town

The statue on the left of the image was begun in 1898 to mark the centenary of the 1798 Rebellion and was unveiled the following year. The year of the rebellion is carved into the flag the figure holds.

The other flags in the picture, and in the one opposite, suggest celebrations marking the end of the First World War. As part of the Empire at the time, many thousands of Irishmen fought with the allies in the fields of France.

Above and right: Castle Street, Sligo Town

Castle Street was probably named after an old Castle or tower house that once stood on its corner with Abbey Street, long since gone. Like most streets it was unofficially named in earlier times, before rules and processes existed to arrange such things.

The building that once housed the Sligo Independent Offices faced the statue seen in the picture above, at the junction with Market Street. It is a simple and plain structure, making use of the local limestone. A pleasing feature was its arched opening on the ground floor, accommodating office and shop, as well as access to the floors above. These have since given way to mundane modern replacements, which are much less in keeping with the building's character. So too are the new windows overhead, which jut out of the window opening in a triangular shape.

On the Estate

Above and opposite: Ferry and Windmill, Hazelwood

These two constructions demonstrate the breadth of estate architecture, and the complexity of ancillary buildings and structures that enabled the smooth running of a large estate. The estate in question is Hazelwood House, constructed in 1731 to the design of Richard Castle. The small ferry (above) follows an almost medieval design, consisting of a floating bridge-like barge that could be used to cross the water – much cheaper than constructing an actual bridge.

The small mill (opposite, above), perched on the water's edge, may have been used to pump water to the main house, rather than to mill corn. The base of it survives today.

Opposite below: Lisheen House, Ballysadare

Originally the house was known as Seafield, and was built in 1842 for the Phibbs family. It was designed by the local architect John Benson and replaced an earlier gothic-revival house nearby. The house was reputedly haunted, which may have had something to do with its name being changed to Lisheen in 1904. The spirits seem to have won out however and the family sold the house in 1940, following which it was immediately dismantled.

Seaside Castle

Above: Cliff Baths, Inishcrone

This delightful structure was once a small bath-house complex, built about 1890, and erected to cater to the needs of visiting tourists when Enniscrone (as it was known) was a popular seaside-holiday destination. It sits on a natural rock foundation and is reached via steps from the main road above. Sadly it is today boarded and blocked up, and beginning to deteriorate. It is to be hoped that such a curious and pretty building will be revived with some new purpose in the future rather than being abandoned completely to the waves.

Above: Tea House, Glencar

Living over the shop is a useful notion, but here the 'shop' is the home. A once-common thatched house takes advantage of the tourist trade by setting up as a Tea House, providing refreshments to those visiting the local dramatic scenery.

Right: Tourist Car, Sligo Town

This horse-drawn 'car' would once have been the tourist coach of its day, transporting people from train station to hotel, to local sights, attractions and places of interest. Waterproof tarpaulins would have been provided to cover the legs and upper body when it rained, which in Ireland is not uncommon.

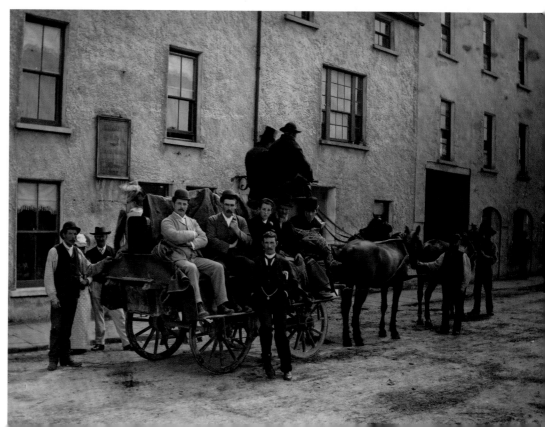

ULSTER

ANTRIM

The county of Antrim lies in the north-east extreme of the island, bounded on two sides, east and north, by the narrow channel of the Irish Sea separating it from Scotland, and to the south-west by Lough Neagh.

The Plantation of Ulster saw the development of many new planned towns in this part of the island, but it was to be the existing settlement of Belfast that would become the centre of wealth and success which would come to dominate not just Antrim, but the whole north-east of the island.

Belfast sits at the mouth of the Lagan valley, and it was here that the business of linen took root and flourished. Up until the mid-eighteenth century linen would have been produced by individuals working in their own homes. Husband and wife would have spun the yarn themselves from their own flax and then have woven it into linen cloth. It was a cottage industry. The coming of the industrial revolution, however, changed all that. The introduction of machinery replaced individuals with factories and mills and linen output grew accordingly. Although originally controlled through merchants in Dublin, bitter disputes in the 1780s caused Belfast merchants to begin exporting themselves. From the 1830s the number of linen mills rapidly grew and by 1873 Belfast was the largest exporter of linen in the world.

It has been suggested that this foothold of the Industrial Revolution was partially responsible for Belfast's other great industry, shipbuilding. Remembered today by its two great shipyards Harland & Wolff and Workman, Clark & Co. These yards grew steadily, producing such impressive ships as the *Olympic*, *Britannia* and, of course, the *Titanic*. They employed thousands of people directly, not to mention the associated jobs they supported in areas like engineering and rope-making.

With the partition of Ireland Belfast became the official capital of Northern Ireland on May 3, 1921.

Following the boom they had experienced during the First World War, production slowed at the shipyards, compounded by the economic slump brought about by the Wall Street Crash in 1929. Workman, Clark & Co was closed in 1935, but Harland & Wolff survived. During the Second World War they were to experience a similar boom. It was partially this success that made Belfast such an inviting target for the Luftwaffe. On both the 15–16 April and 4–5 May 1941 the city was blitzed. 850 people were killed, 1,600 homes destroyed, 28,000 houses damaged, and 15,000 people left homeless. The devastation of the war was compounded by the collapse of the world market for linen in the 1950s with a consequent surge in poverty and unemployment.

The Troubles of the 1970s, 80s and 90s wrecked havoc of another kind on the city. One third of the population left Belfast, with more than 50% leaving from the centre of the city. Although much has changed for the better today, the following pages record some of what has been lost over the previous decades.

Opposite: Pilot Office, Belfast Harbour
An unusual little building consisting of a circular parapet resting on an octagonal tower, resulting in the pleasing triangular pattern formed around the top. It stood at the entrance to Spencer Dock on the north side of the River Lagan. In the background is the shipyard of the firm Workman Clarke.

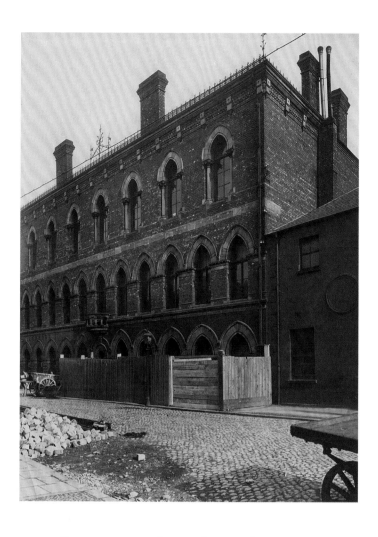

Opposite above: Bedford Street, Belfast

A combination of size and pared-back, elegant details, made Bedford Street typical of the Industrial Revolution architecture in Britain, but it was a combination that appeared little in Ireland, with the exception of Belfast. The somewhat stern nature of the street had its own beauty. Most of its buildings have since been replaced with modern office structures, of which Windsor House, at 23 storeys, is the most massive. It occupies the site just opposite the domed corner seen on the left of the image.

Opposite below: Royal Victoria Hospital, Belfast

The hospital was completed to the designs of Henman & Cooper and was opened by King Edward VII in 1903. This wing consisted of 17 wards, connected by a long corridor. They have since been subsumed by the hospital's necessity to expand.

Left: St Lennon's Catholic Repository, Queen Street, Belfast

The Catholic Repository was designed by Anthony Thomas Jackson and constructed about 1870. It was a working-men's club housed behind a rhythmic façade of Victorian gothic arches. It was demolished in 1915.

Below: Belfast Boat Club, Lockview Road, Belfast

A quaint Victorian pavilion that provided some light relief to the industrial rigour of most of Belfast, the Boat Club was opened in 1897. The Belfast Boat Club still occupies the site, but the Club House itself was destroyed by an IRA bomb in 1972.

Industrial Rhythm

Bridging the Divide

Above and left: Bridges, Belfast

Along with factories and railways, bridges were one of the key achievements of the Industrial Revolution. Queen's Bridge (left) was designed by John Frazer and Charles Lanyon and opened in 1843. It was named after Queen Victoria and was later widened with the addition of cantilevered footpaths in the 1880s. Albert Bridge was designed by J.C. Bretland and opened in 1890. It was named after Victoria's grandson, who had laid the foundation stone a few years earlier.

Both bridges as seen here are set in the heart of an industrial wonderland, the horizons dotted with chimneys and factories. They themselves were the product of their dynamic times, and both survive today. The cityscape they served to link, however, has changed markedly. In the place of chimneys and factories are today high-rise office blocks and apartment complexes.

Middle-Class Metropolis

Above: Castle Place, Belfast

The busy commercial heart of the city would have provided a wealth of possibilities for those with the means to shop. Although the centre of the city suffered during the blitz, the large department store of J. Rob & Co, seen curving around the corner in the middle of the image, survived the war. It had been built in the 1870s and traded right up until 1973, when it closed. It was eventually demolished in 1991 and replaced with a rather plain and uninteresting 'development'.

Left: Shaftsbury Square, Belfast

Shaftsbury Square was once a neat but busy intersection of several roads and streets in the city. This image shows the Magdalen School, the church-like building with a tower to its left placed between two streets. It was designed by Charles Lanyon in 1853. Like much of the square it has been replaced, and what survives is almost unrecognisable.

Above: Temporary Arch, Donegall Place, Belfast

This temporary arch was erected for a royal visit, probably one paid by King Edward VII in 1903 or 1907. Such constructions followed in a long tradition of temporary triumphal arches erected for visiting celebrities or heroes. It is remarkable to think it was only ever intended for one occasion. It is decorated with the symbols of Belfast's industrial prosperity, notably the spinning wheel which crowns the top of it. Through the arch can be seen the old White Linen Hall (p. 306).

Right: Wellington Place, Belfast

Decorated shop fronts like this were indicative of a prosperous middle class that would have thrived amongst the wealth of the large industrial city. This particular one is composed of terracotta and glazed tiles, intended to make an impression on passers-by. Although still standing, it appears to have been disregarded long ago and has been left to the devices of those who don't seem to fully appreciate it.

Power and Might

Right: High Street, Belfast

High Street was typical of the commercial might of Belfast in its prime. Impressive buildings, in local red-hued sandstone, were highly ornamented. A sizeable part of the street was destroyed during the blitz. Today what remains is a patchwork of original buildings being slowly overshadowed by new concrete neighbours. The Albert Clock of 1869, closing the street, still stands.

Below: Harbour, Belfast

Shipbuilding was the foundation of Belfast's industrial prowess. This photograph of the S.S. *Viper* shows an infrastructure of rhythmic brick along the harbour's edge. It was this prowess and infrastructure that made the shipyards of Belfast a prime target for bombers during the Second World War. In later decades, with the waning of the ship construction trade, such buildings that had survived gave way to modern developments.

Opposite both: Victoria Barracks, Belfast

The first military barracks was established on this site in the late 1700s. Over the years it grew in importance, being added to and extended along the way until it was almost entirely rebuilt in the 1880s. It is from that time that most of the buildings in these two images date, resplendent in their dour Victorian rigidity. The barracks was renamed after Queen Victoria following her death in 1901. It was dismantled from the 1960s onwards and the area redeveloped as housing.

Above: G.N.R. Terminus, Great Victoria Street, Belfast

The first railway station in Belfast opened on this site in 1839 and was later replaced with the building shown here, to the designs of John Godwin, in 1848. It was a grand, imperial-looking edifice, somewhat obscured by its own canopy at the front. It was closed in 1976 and later demolished, only for a new train station to be built in 1995, when it was decided that it was a necessary part of the city's infrastructure.

Industrial Prowess

Opposite below: N.C.R. Terminus, York Street, Belfast

The Northern Counties Railway station was built to the designs of the architect Charles Lanyon in the middle of the nineteenth century. It suffered a violent history, being bombed in the 1941 blitz and later in the 1970s during the Troubles. It was closed in 1975 and shortly afterward demolished. It has since been replaced with a modest brown-brick station building.

Right above: Lunatic Asylum, Falls Road, Belfast

This District Lunatic Asylum was designed by the architect William Murray in 1826 and opened in 1829, capable of accommodating one hundred patients. It was extended several times thereafter, notably by Charles Lanyon in the early 1850s. It was demolished in 1924.

Below left and right: Linen

The driving engine of Belfast was its linen factories. Ewart's Linen Factory on the Crumlin Road (below right) gives some idea of the complicated machinery that was housed within the massive brick and iron structures that employed thousands and exported across the globe.

The York Street Flax Spinning Company (below left) was, on the eve of its destruction, the largest of its kind in the world. Both establishments were casualties of the Luftwaffe in 1941.

Beyond the City

Above: Antrim Castle, Antrim

The first castle was begun here by Sir Hugh Clotworthy in 1612, and further enlarged by his son in 1662. It was entirely rebuilt between 1813 and 1818 to the designs of the architect John Bowden, who retained the original seventeenth-century door surround, which rose to three storeys and can be seen in the image above. It was further enlarged in 1887 and destroyed by fire in 1922. The ruins stood until their demolition in the 1970s, but the magnificent gardens still survive.

Opposite above: Cave Hill, Newtownabbey

Cave Hill, to the north of the city of Belfast, was a popular destination for day-trippers, offering as it did expansive views over the city.

Opposite below: Cave House, Cushendall

A completely unexpected construction, utilising the natural rock formation as part of its structure, this is the kind of house more associated with the arid climate of places like Turkey. It displays the ingenuity of the vernacular builder. When even the most basic of structures might have been too much to afford, this solution utilised what was already available and cut down on the number of walls needed and the labour required to build them.

Work and Play

Left: Imperial Hotel, Donegall Place, Belfast

The Imperial Hotel was the property of Mr H. Jury, whose name is still synonymous with hotels in Ireland today. It originally occupied a building that had been the residence of one Hugh Montgomery. This was renovated in 1868, when the architect Charles Acton Sherry added two storeys to it and renovated the existing structure. It was demolished in 1959.

Below: White Linen Hall, Donegall Square, Belfast

Constructed between 1782 and 1785, this large but relatively modest building was the heart of the linen trade in Ulster. It was designed by Roger Mulholland and consisted of four ranges of two storeys enclosing a large quad. This image shows a view toward the main entrance from within the enclosure. It was demolished to make way for Belfast City Hall in 1896. That impressive monument still occupies the site today.

Above: Royal Hippodrome, Great Victoria Street, Belfast
The Royal Hippodrome opened next to the Belfast Opera House in 1907. It was designed by Bertie Crewe and continued to operate via a variety of owners up until its demolition in 1998. In the early 1960s its exterior was clad in metal to give it a modern 'lift'. It was damaged by an IRA bomb in 1974 and became a bingo hall in 1987. The Opera House, to the left in the picture, still survives.

Right: Theatre Royal, Arthur Square, Belfast
A theatre stood at this site as far back as 1793. This first building was replaced by the one shown, in 1871, to the designs of Charles Sherry, which was built by Lanyon, Lynn & Lanyon. It sadly didn't last long. It was destroyed by fire on June 8, 1881 and a new theatre rebuilt and reopened on the same site in the remarkable space of just six months. It, in turn, was demolished in 1915.

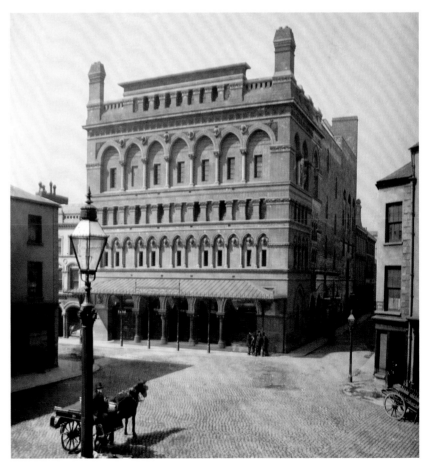

ARMAGH

Armagh is traditionally the place where St Patrick founded his church in Ireland and to this day it is the ecclesiastical capital of the Island, seat of the Roman Catholic and Church of Ireland Primates of All Ireland, each titled the Archbishop of Armagh. The city itself is quite fine. The hill on which St Patrick's church stood is now the site of the Church of Ireland cathedral, faced from another hill nearby by the Roman Catholic cathedral of the same name. It can lead to some confusion.

The county at large is mountainous towards its southern end, gradually sloping through the Drumlin belt towards Lough Neagh, to what Lewis, in his topographical directory of 1837, describes as 'gentle swells and fertile vales'.

Following the eruption of 'the Troubles' in Northern Ireland in the late 1960s, Armagh became a hotbed of fighting to the extent that the south of the county became known as 'bandit country'. It was a place of staunch Republicanism, centered around towns like Crossmaglen and Jonesborough, close to the border with the Republic. Such was the level of threat and hostility that the local army barracks at Crossmaglen had everything, down to mail and newspapers, delivered by helicopter.

Within this context, Tynan Abbey, and the circumstances of its destruction, may possibly be the bloodiest incident related in these pages. The house itself was originally constructed for one John Stronge, curate of Tynan in about 1750. A descendent, Matthew,

was made Baronet Stronge in 1803 in return for his supporting the Union and, about 1815–20 the existing house was enlarged, almost certainly by John Nash. The family were great Unionists (Sir James Stronge, 6th Baronet, being Imperial Grand Master of the Loyal Orange Lodge until his death in 1928) and the house eventually made its way to Sir Norman Lockhart Stronge. Sir Norman had a long career in politics. He was first elected to the Northern Ireland House of Commons in 1938, and from 1945 until his retirement in 1969 served as its Speaker.

On the evening of January 21, 1981, 86-year-old Sir Norman and his son James, 48, were sitting watching television in the library at Tynan Abbey. It was one of the few rooms of their vast mansion that they continued to inhabit. Members of the provisional IRA arrived, blowing the doors open with a grenade. Sir Norman sent up a flare to alert the authorities, but it was too late. The bodies of both he and his son, with bullet wounds to their heads, were recovered from the burning house when the security forces arrived shortly after. The perpetrators had bombed the house and set it alight before making their getaway. It was completely gutted. It stood as a gaunt ruin and a grim reminder of more troubled times until all but a doorway was demolished in 1998 following concerns for the structural safety of the surviving ruin.

Opposite: Train Station, Portadown
Truly imperial in scale, this long, grand structure epitomized the golden age of the railways in the Victorian world. It was designed by James MacNeill and built between 1861 and 1862. It served its purpose, splendidly, until it was demolished in 1970.

Ancient Footholds

Right: Governor's House, Charlemont Fort, Armagh

Charlemont Fort dates to 1602 when it was constructed by Charles Blount, Lord Mountjoy. Its Governor's house was a charming lodge, with clusters of chimneys on the corners and projections on each façade lending it a truly animated and picturesque appearance. It was destroyed by fire in 1920 and the ruins soon after demolished.

Below left: Carrickblacker Castle, Portadown

The home of the Blacker family dated to 1692, but it was extensively altered in the nineteenth century with the addition of a curving Dutch-style gable and balustrade parapet, among other things. The result, seen here, was somewhat clunky, but nonetheless possessing a naive charm. The estate was sold to Portadown Golf Club who eventually demolished the house in 1988 to make way for a new clubhouse.

Below right: Ballymoyer House, Belleek

Ballymoyer House was a three-storey house built in the eighteenth century to which a new wing, almost a new house, was added at right angles in the first half of the nineteenth century, the two together forming a 'T' on plan. Here we see the new addition to the house. It was demolished in the first half of the twentieth century and the estate later gifted to the National Trust.

Opposite: Gough Barracks, Armagh

Gough Barracks, named after the famous Field Marshal, Hugh, 1st Viscount Gough, was begun in 1773, replacing an earlier barracks in the town. Like many such compounds it was enlarged substantially over the years. During the Second World War it was home to US soldiers. It was vacated by the army in 1976, around which time many of its buildings were demolished.

Embracing the Street

Opposite: Armagh Post Office, English Street, Armagh

An elegant building in the classical idiom, housing a large, well-lit hall at ground-floor level, much like a bank. It has been replaced in the latter half of the twentieth century, by an almost offensively uninteresting structure, that today accommodates the post office.

Above left: 59 Scotch Street, Armagh

A neat, unpretentious building, somehow both organised and yet fantastically chaotic. Typical of Victorian and Edwardian tastes. The building survives. When last I came across it, it was home to a fast-food shop.

Above right: Armagh & District Co-operative Society, Thomas Street, Armagh

Constructed in 1903, the home of the co-operative society was an ornamental if somewhat restrained structure that was crowned by an elegant parapet. The building was demolished and replaced with one that attempts to replicate it but fails, badly. It begs the question, why wasn't the original just retained?

Aristocratic Heft

All: Drumbanagher House, Poyntzpass

Drumbanagher was an incredibly robust house, designed by the Scottish architect James Playfair in 1829. It was Italianate in style, constructed of sandstone shipped over from Scotland, and when completed, formed an 'H' in plan. The central block had a wing either side, and between the two projections at the front was a massive port-cochère, a covered area from which to alight from your carriage (below right). From the rear the house overlooked terraces leading down to a large ornamental body of water (right).

The grandiose exterior was equally matched by the interior, the impressive library of which can be seen here (below left).

The house was occupied by British and American soldiers during the Second World War. Following this the owners decided it was not financially feasible to maintain it and, although in perfectly sound condition, it was demolished in 1951. Only the port-cochère remains today to give any idea of its original scale.

Above: The Square, Armagh

The east side of the Market Square in Armagh was once home to these four eclectic nineteenth-century houses. In much the same way that Georgian town houses follow a similar pattern but are individually different, so these four buildings all shared common features while maintaining their individuality. None now survives, their sites now home to a row of unremarkable buildings in dull brown brick.

Above: Tynan Abbey, Tynan

Although an actual abbey never occupied the site, the name reflected the ideas of the picturesque and the romantic popular at the time of its remodelling in the 1820s. It was one of the more successful gothic-revival constructions, convincingly appearing as a mixture of different additions from different times. It was destroyed in a vicious IRA attack in 1981 and the runs later demolished.

Opposite above left: Drummilly House, Loughgall

Drummilly was a bizarre house. Its stretched-out frontage with narrow central block looked almost institutional in its form and plainness. However, projecting from the centre of this oddity was an even greater one, an utterly unexpected oval, art nouveau conservatory. This delightful structure, with pivoting oval windows and rounded roof, acted as the main entrance. Neither house nor art nouveau oval survive.

Walls of Glass

Above right: Milford House, Armagh

Milford was built for the McCrum family and radically remodelled in 1880 by the firm of Young and Mackenzie. It had an astonishing amount of plumbing, including hot and cold water and baths, for its time. It was also lit with electric lights, supplied by hydroelectric power. Another unusual feature was the large conservatory extending from the main building. The family fell on hard times following the Wall Street Crash. In 1936 the house became a school and a new wing was added in 1964. It later became a hospital and, although vacant and boarded up, survives today.

Left: The Pavilion, Armagh

An incongruous mix of styles and forms, the whole of the Pavilion looks like a large conservatory from a distance. It was built for one Captain W.W. Alego around 1820 and among its curiosities was a gothic-revival doorway shielded by a classical portico, a large conservatory to the right and a trellised arcade to the left. It was rented by a group of Sacred Heart nuns while their convent was being built, between 1851 and 1857. Later it was occupied by allied soldiers during the Second World War. Following the war it was demolished.

CAVAN

Cavan is well known today as Ireland's lake district. The county presents a sparse, bubbling landscape of Drumlin hills, surrounded by lakes and waterways of every shape and size, gradually becoming more mountainous as one moves further north-west. It is reputed there are three hundred and sixty five lakes spread across the county – one for each day of the year. It is only appropriate therefore that it is from here that the great border between east and west begins: the River Shannon rises from a large, dark circular pool known as the 'Shannon Pot' and from here begins its steady journey south, bisecting the island.

This landscape of hills and large expanses of water lent itself naturally to defence and the remains of many ancient forts and tombs are scattered throughout the county. This part of the island, with Leitrim, was originally part of the old Irish kingdom of Breffni until it was officially 'shired' in 1584, becoming the County of Cavan we know today. Soon after the county was 'planted' during the Ulster Plantation, at which time many new planned towns appeared, among them Virginia, Bailieborough, Belturbet and Kingscourt.

The county is dotted with fine architecture, the outstanding example of which is Bellamont Forest, designed by Sir Edward Lovett Pearce. At the time of writing it is currently vacant and beginning to show the effects of neglect and water damage.

Some of Cavan's other architectural gems have sadly met with worse fates and no longer survive at all. Of these one of the more interesting was Annaghlee. Attributed to Richard Castle, pupil of Sir Edward Lovett Pearce, this was a much more modest house, also of redbrick, than Bellamont.

The loss of houses such as Annaghlee (opposite, also pp. 326–27) is all the sadder given their scale and 'livability'. Although falling under the label of 'big house' neither was all that large. By modern standards they would have been considered quite manageable and well suited to modern family life. Sadly it was, and still is, often the case that the lure of modern comforts often outweighs the genuine cost of maintaining such old buildings. In some cases they have been abandoned simply because they seemed old-fashioned and archaic, throwbacks to an age where they represented much more than the simple, refined work of native Irish hands.

Opposite: Annaghlee House, Cootehill
The harmonious proportions and modest scale of Annaghlee provide an unpretentious backdrop to the daily grind of country life.

Tradition Celebrated

Opposite: Healy's Bar, Main Street, Virginia

The pub, and the rest of the Main Street, here decorated for the wedding of the local landlord, Lord Headford, in the early twentieth century. Such decorations had a long traditional heritage. The buildings survive, though much chopped and changed today.

Above: Mill Cottages, Dublin Road, Virginia

The cottages stood next to the mill on the Dublin Road, the archway and gable wall of which can be seen behind the cart of the left. The mill is still extant, but the quiet, snug composition of three thatched homes has since been moved.

The Moving Cathedral

Above and right: Old Roman Catholic Cathedral, Farnham Street, Cavan

In 1823 a new stone structure replaced an earlier thatched Catholic church on this site on Farnham Street. It in turn was extended between 1853 and 1862, when a new nave and chancel (right) were added at right angles to the 1823 building, which became the transepts of this new arrangement. Following this work the church became the Cathedral of St Patrick and St Felim. It remained as such until it was replaced by the modern-day cathedral in 1947. It was then dismantled and re-erected in Ballyhaise (without its transepts) where it was demolished in 1952 and the stone used to build the Church of St Mary at Castlerea.

Above: Castle Saunderson, Belturbet

The home of the Saunderson family was built in the late seventeenth century and remodelled in the mid 1830s by one George Sudden, who transformed it into a gothic 'castle'. It was sold in 1977 and later used as a hotel before being damaged by fire. It is today boarded up. The grounds were recently opened as an international scouting centre.

Right: Bailieborough Castle, Bailieborough

The 'castle' at Bailieborough may have dated to 1629, when the Scottish planter Sir William Bailie constructed a house on the site. It was altered, giving it its castle-like appearance, by Sir John Young, later 1st Baron Lisger and Governor General of Canada. It was sold in 1918 to a religious group, the Marist Brothers, damaged by fire in 1918 and eventually demolished by its new owner, the Land Commission, shortly after it acquired it in 1936.

Municipal Cornerstones

Opposite above: Main Street, Cavan

Neat rows of houses make up the Main Street seen here. The narrower the plots along a street the more there are, adding to the subtle variety of the streetscape and creating a certain 'grain'. Sadly, like many streets across the island, several of these small plots have been cleared and joined together to allow for the creation of an invariably overwhelming and middling piece of speculative building in the form of a shopping centre or apartment/office block. Cavan's Main Street has sadly become home to several examples.

Below left and right: Holy Trinity Church, Kildoagh

One of the finest just-about surviving examples of a traditional barn-like Catholic church, built in 1796. It was enlivened on the exterior in the later nineteenth century and continued in use up until 1979. It is now vacant and without a purpose. It sorely needs one if it is not to be lost to future generations.

Above: Market House, Main Street, Cavan

Cavan has always been a busy market town. This structure was originally the court house, built in 1827, and was converted into a market house in 1855 on the orders of the local landlord, Lord Farnham. It has since been replaced.

Sophisticated Masculinity

Above: Lismore Castle, Crossdoney

Lismore was built about 1730, possibly to the designs of the well-known architect Edward Lovett Pearce. Pearce was related to the English architect John Vanbrugh, and the house certainly suggests a familiarity with his work in its massing and masculinity. It was vacated around 1870 and in 1952 the central block, shown here, was demolished with the exception of one of the small 'towers' seen to left and right. Also surviving are two large wings, not visible in this image here.

Right and opposite: Annaghlee House, Cootehill

Annaghlee was a beautiful house, of average size and perfectly proportioned. It was built around 1750 for one Robert Wills, possibly to the designs of Richard Castle. It was not very big, from the front appearing slightly raised up on a basement which opened fully into a yard at the rear. It was abandoned in the twentieth century.

LONDONDERRY

Derry takes its name from its city, which originally grew up around the monastic community of St Colmcille, in turn taken over and settled by the Vikings. It was redeveloped during the plantation of Ulster by City of London livery companies and accordingly, in 1613, received its prefix of 'London'. Its history has meant its name can be a contentious issue and although known by many as 'Derry', officially its name is recorded as 'Londonderry'.

Politics aside, the city itself is remarkable in being the only intact surviving walled settlement in Ireland. Its famous walls were never breached, despite several attempts and sieges. The most famous of these came about in 1689, when the Apprentice Boys locked the gates of the city against the advancing army of King James II. The siege that followed lasted 105 days and was one of the defining events of the Williamite wars. Later, during the eighteenth and nineteenth centuries, many fine buildings were added to the city, some of which have not made it to the twenty-first century.

Beyond the city the landscape is one of gentle river valleys that rise to the moors of the Sperrin Mountains in the south, and skirt around these towards the shores of Lough Neagh in the east. To the north the coast is harried by the waves of the Atlantic. Here, perched on a remote cliff top, are the remains of one of Northern Ireland's greatest houses, Downhill.

Downhill was begun in the 1770s by one of the most colourful figures of the eighteenth century, Frederick Augustus Hervey, known to posterity as 'the Earl-Bishop.' Hervey was the third of four sons and therefore not likely to succeed to the family title. He made a career for himself in the church and, with the aid of his family connections, gained for himself the See of Derry. Shortly afterwards he succeeded to the earldom of Bristol following the death of his elder brothers. Downhill was just one of his many architectural adventures, and probably the most reserved – from the outside at least. Its interiors were filled with the plunder of his grand tour in Italy, and decorated accordingly. His other houses were quite similar to each other. Of these no trace of Ballyscullion survives, while Ickworth House in Suffolk, England is today managed and opened to the public by the National Trust. It gives the best idea of Hervey's architectural playfulness and pretention as it would have appeared at Ballyscullion.

Following the Earl-Bishop Downhill suffered fire and repair, and survived the tumult of the revolutionary period of 1919–21 before being commandeered as a billet for RAF officers during the Second World War. Derry was on the western cusp of allied territory and it, with Lough Foyle, became an important U.S. Naval Operation base. Following the war the house was unroofed and exposed to the elements, much as one still finds it today.

Opposite: Londonderry City
General view over the city of Derry/Londonderry from the south bank of the River Foyle.

Above and right: Great Northern Railway Station, Foyle Road, Derry/ Londonderry

This station was the main terminus of the Londonderry to Enniskillen Railway line. It opened in 1850 and was designed by the partnership of Thomas Turner and Richard Williamson. It was a relatively pared-back Italianate design, constructed of red brick. The last train departed the platforms, with their elegant and industrial iron canopies, in 1965 and a large part of the site was subsequently demolished in 1970. Part of what remains is today a Railway Museum.

Victorian Innovations

Left: National Schools, Kilrea

This handsome block was designed by the architect William Barnes and constructed in 1864. It follows traditional thinking at the time, consisting of two wings, one for girls and one for boys. The separate wings are joined by an entrance in the middle and each of the three main elements is clearly distinguished.

Below: Bann Bridge, Colerain

In this view, looking east, are clearly visible the town's main landmarks, the Town Hall and the church. While these survive, much else has disappeared, not least the ship moored by the riverside.

The Religious Influence

Above left: YMCA building, East Wall, Derry/Londonderry

The Young Men's Christian Association was constructed to the designs of J.G. Ferguson between 1866 and 1867 on the site of the old Linen Hall. In 1891 it was enlarged by the addition of a gymnasium to the rear. It remained standing while all around it was demolished in the early 1970s, finally giving way in 1980. It, and its neighboring sites, are today home to the Millennium Forum.

Above right: St Columb's Celebrations, Derry/Londonderry

These street decorations were erected for the St Columb's celebrations. St Columb (or St Columba) founded the settlement here on the banks of the River Foyle that eventually became the city of Derry/Londonderry. The saint is featured over the arch, which is surmounted by a Celtic cross. Such decorations were only ever temporary.

Opposite: Waterloo Place, Derry/Londonderry

This image shows Waterloo Place, looking north-west, just outside the great city walls, which are visible to the left. All of the buildings in the centre of the image have since been replaced, and the celebrated Northern Counties Hotel of 1899 has yet to be constructed.

The Famous Walls

Above: Walker Monument, Grand Parade, Derry/Londonderry
The Rev. George Walker was one of the heroes of Unionism, having been appointed governor of the city during its infamous siege from 1688 to 1689. In 1828 a carved statue of him, nine feet high, was placed atop a 96 foot high column. The statue was carved by the sculptor John Smyth and the column contained spiral stairs that gave access to a viewing platform on the top. It was blown up by a 100lb bomb in 1973.

Above: Eel Fishing, Kilrea

Eel was once a common foodsource along this stretch of the River Bann. Although no longer popular locally, eel is still a large source of income for many families in the area today as an export.

Right: Straidarran House, Claudy

A deceptively large villa, elevated above the surrounding landscape on a raised basement. The hipped roof hides another floor above, making this three-storey house appear more a one-floor 'cottage'.

The Busy Street

Opposite above: Ferryquay Street, Derry/Londonderry

The bustling activity of this street is reflected in the buildings that line it, robust and utilitarian but accentuated with a Victorian fondness for detail and variety. Much of the streetscape has since been replaced.

Opposite below: Gaol, Bishop's St, Derry/Londonderry

This magnificent structure was constructed to the designs of Edward Miller in 1791. It was the third gaol in the city, replacing an earlier one located on Ferryquay Street. Prisoners over the years included Wolfe Tone and Éamon de Valera. All but one tower was demolished in the 1970s as part of a redevelopment scheme.

Left: Queen's Quay Shipping Office, Derry/Londonderry

An ornamented, utilitarian building in the Italianate style, the shipping office was a reminder of the city's importance as a port. The tracks laid in the cobbles and the crane on the right also bore evidence to this.

Below: McMaster's Pub, Maghera

A typical pub in the vernacular tradition, it likely evolved over time from its original function as a house. The large windows on the ground floor are indicative of its earlier use as a shop, in the time before the development of shopfronts.

Building Bishops

Opposite: Downhill Castle, Coleraine

Downhill began life as a small eighteenth-century villa, built of local basalt, for the Earl-Bishop of Derry, Frederick Hervey. Over the course of its complicated building history the names of some of the most prominent architects of the time make an appearance, including John Soane, Robert Adam and James Wyatt. Yet it was local Irish architects and masons who are largely credited with the rather austere house seen here.

In 1851 most of the house was destroyed by fire and wasn't rebuilt until some 20 years later. The Earl-Bishop's gallery, (below) was given new life as a winter garden in this rebuilding and reorganisation. Following requisition during the Second World War the house was stripped of its roof and left.

Above: 27 Bishop Street, Derry/Londonderry

Located just within the city walls, next to the Bishop's Gate, these stables once served the adjacent palace of the Bishop of Derry, the top of which can be seen just over the central pediment. They were demolished sometime in the 1970s to make way for an army barracks, which stood on the site until 2005. The barracks is now gone and the site, with the remains of the palace gardens, is now a car park.

DONEGAL

On approaching the city of Derry in 1837, Charlotte Elizabeth Tonna described the view of Donegal which she could see on the other side of the Foyle river as a 'long, regular, undulating line of mountain tops' which 'seemed endless'. This view of Donegal is romantically accurate. It is a place stark, barren and bleak in its natural beauty, battered by the noisy Atlantic along much of its jagged perimeter. But in between these 'endless' mountains one finds sheltered dells and dales that provide a respite from the elements, offering a foothold against the harsh realities of Nature.

The county is undoubtedly the most isolated in Ireland, and this relative remove from the centres of power allowed its lords to consolidate their influence. In Irish it is sometimes known as 'Tír Chonaill', the 'land of Conall', whose descendants, the O'Donnells, were one of Ireland's richest and most powerful old Gaelic families. Their influence came to an end with the Flight of the Earls in 1607, when the Earl of Tyrconnell (as he was styled under the English system) and Hugh O'Neill, the Earl of Tyrone, departed Ireland with their families. They made their way to the Catholic courts of Europe to seek assistance in their struggle against the English, but they never returned.

The county has always been famed for its beautiful landscape, and with the arrival of the railways, many more people were able to admire it. Railways, and the tourism they brought with them, made an important impact on the county. Many hotels sprang up to cater to the needs of these new visitors and to take advantage of their largess. Beyond the guesthouse however, life here was hard, and the cottages of the poor reflect both the belligerence of the climate and the paucity of local materials from which to construct a home. Some were literally made of sods of earth.

Larger houses were, and are, present too, a particular favourite of the author's being Wardtown House, near Ballyshannon. It was built about 1740 for a Colonel Folliott, evidently a gentleman of learning given what he had constructed. Even in its current state of ruination it presents an aspect more fortress-like than domestic, perhaps conscious of defending its inhabitants against the Atlantic gales. Its bowed projections suggest towers and its whole front is rigorously symmetrical. This fortitude did not lessen the interior comforts, tantalising glimpses of which were, until recently, still possible. The house appears to have been inhabited until about 1916 by one Ellie Likely, after which it was abandoned and, given its exposure no doubt, quickly fell into ruin. The Land Commission eventually split the estate up in the 1930s and what remains of the house, although today in ruin, is still quite impressive.

Opposite: Wardtown House, Ballyshannon
The bowed projections on the front of Wardtown House presenting a Bastille-like appearance to the elements.

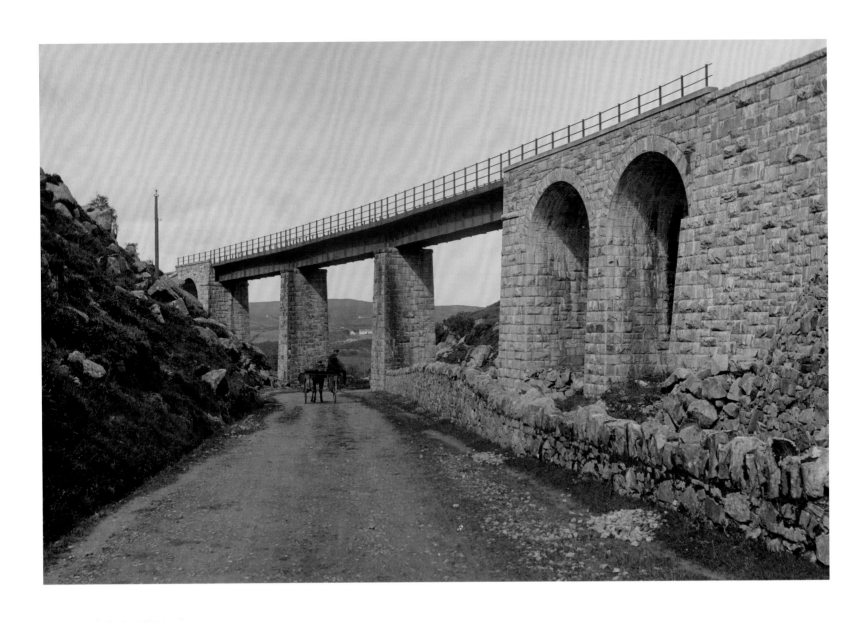

Opening Up

Above: Barnes Gap Viaduct, Creeslough

The railways went a huge way to opening up this most remote of Ireland's corners in the late nineteenth and early twentieth centuries. At one point the county boasted 225 miles of track, which today has been reduced to just three. Of the viaduct here at Barnes Gap, only the piers remain, the span having been removed in the 1940s.

Left: Owencarrow Viaduct, Drumnacarry

This impressive viaduct, built in 1903, is well known for the disaster that happened on it in 1925. During stormy conditions wind caused several carriages to leave the tracks, resulting in four people dropping to their deaths. The route it was part of, Letterkenny to Burtonport, saw its last train run in 1941 and the line was closed in 1947. Only the piers remain today.

Above: Camlin Castle, Camlin

Camlin began life as a house built around 1718 for the family of Tredennick. It was greatly altered and extended to the designs of the architect John B. Keane about 1838, creating a Tudor-revival mansion that incorporated parts of the old house to the rear. It was sold to the Land Commission at the turn of the century and was demolished by the Electricity Supply Board a few decades later in the mistaken belief that it would be submerged by a hydro-electric scheme. In the event the water never rose so high.

Right: Ballymacool House, Letterkenny

Originally a typical five-bay, two-storey house of the Georgian period, Ballymacool was constructed about 1770 for the Boyd family. It was transformed around 1830 into the Tudor-revival mansion seen perched on the hill here. It survived occupation by Republican soldiers in 1921 to be sold in 1940. It is now a ruin following a relatively recent fire.

Timeless

Right: Train Station, Stranorlar

The train station at Stranorlar opened in 1863 and later became the headquarters of the Donegal railway company. It closed in 1960 and was later demolished to make way for the current bus depot. The old station clock has been restored and placed in a modern structure on the site.

Below: General View, Ballyshannon

The town of Ballyshannon as seen here from across the River Erne would not have changed much from late medieval times in its general form and layout. The old bridge, seen on the left, has since been replaced and the town has expanded beyond its boundaries.

Opposite above: RC Church of the Sacred Heart, Carndonagh

Opposite below: Market House, Carndonagh

Carndonagh is one of the most northerly towns on the island, and even today is relatively isolated. It experienced a brief improvement in fortunes with the arrival of the railway in 1907, but that was closed in 1935. The image (above) shows the demolition of its original Roman Catholic church as the current, vast structure neared completion in 1945. Such confidence had ebbed away several decades later when the Market House on the town's diamond was dismantled (below right).

Burgeoning Tourism

Left and above right: Great Northern Hotel, Bundoran

The railway arrived in Bundoran in 1868 and in 1894 an hotel was built to the design of the architect Thomas Drew for the Great Northern Railway. The hotel bore the name of its parent railway company and was erected to capitalise on the tourism trade, providing many facilities for visitors (right). Bundoran became incredibly popular as a seaside holiday destination with the improvement in transport. The hotel survives, albeit much altered and extended.

Middle right: Glencolumbkille Hotel, Carrick

Another example of the facilities that sprang up to cater to the new trade in tourism, this hotel is really more of a guest house in size and appears to have been several buildings that were later connected to each other. It was much more charming, though not quite as dramatically situated as the Great Northern Hotel.

Below: Lisfannon Golf Links, Buncranna

One of the main leisure pursuits when on holiday was golf, and people travelled to this part of the world to enjoy the game almost as much as they do today. Note the sheep, perhaps employed to keep the grass trim.

Catching the Atlantic Winds

Below: Windmill, Ballindrait

This windmill, built in 1874, is indicative of the light touch the Industrial Revolution laid on Ireland generally. Although large factory complexes like those in Britain were rare outside of Belfast, the benefits of the Revolution were felt in smaller enterprises like mills. The mill tower itself survives today, but without its mechanism that once made it so vital a part of local life and commerce.

Opposite above: Mount Tilly, Main Street, Buncrana

This delightful terrace of houses was likely built about 1717 when the town of Buncrana was laid out. In form they are plain vernacular houses with simple A-roofs, but to the front they have incredibly dynamic facades – two-storey derivations of 'proper' town houses of the time that would have been seen in places like Dublin. Quite literally they are a screen of pretention behind which are ordinary houses. One interesting feature is the stairs leading to a first-floor entrance. They seem to have been demolished in the 1930s.

Opposite below: Cottage, Derrybeg

The grimness of this scene of a family, evicted from their home, which has been boarded up, is matched only by the starkness of the house itself. Stone walls with no white lime-wash and a roof that seems to be a patchwork of thatch, heather and sods reflect both the sparseness of the local environment as well as the poverty of everyday life there.

Simple Pleasures

Left: Donegal Cottage Industries

Two ladies sit outside their house, the one on the left 'carding' and the one on the right spinning. Cottage industries, such as spinning wool and lace-making were encouraged in the late nineteenth and early twentieth centuries as a means of providing employment to young women and an additional means of support to families. The simplicity of their house behind them reveals life at the time to have been quite basic.

Below: Moyagh House, Ramelton

A charming, if slightly stern, Victorian villa built in 1878 by the architect J.G. Ferguson. It was L-shaped in plan, the space between the arms being filled by a veranda. In this case it was composed of parts of the railway station at Strabane. The house was destroyed by a fire in 1912 and rebuilt, within its original walls, thereafter.

Above: Circus, Pound Street, Carndonagh

All of the life and variety of the circus is reflected in the quirky painted façade of the building in the background. The fact that it reveals itself as a little disorganised when looked at closely only adds to its charm. In many places it was paint that was the cheapest and easiest way of adding some interest to an otherwise plain building.

DOWN

On his arrival in the county of Down in 1842, J. Stirling Coyne described it as 'a happy combination of mountain, of lowland, of wood and water.' Rocky outcrops and the Mourne Mountains to the south serve as an appropriate demarcation between north and south of the island, to the east is the great inlet of water known as Strangford Lough, and to the north is the city of Belfast, spilling over the border from County Antrim.

In 432AD St Patrick is said to have arrived in Ireland at a place called Saul on the shores of Strangford Lough. Many places across the island claim some association with the Saint, through ancient legends and deeds supposedly done by him in each locality. Downpatrick, a short distance away, is said to be the place where he is buried, lying interred beneath Cathedral Hill and the present day Cathedral Church, alongside St Bridget and St Colmcille.

Newry is one such saint-associated place. Legend has it St Patrick planted a yew tree at the head of Carlingford Lough, around which the town grew up. The name 'Newry' comes from the Gaelic meaning 'yew at the head of the strand'. Whatever the truth behind this, it is one of the oldest towns in Ireland. It grew up around a Cistercian monastery, later emerging as a prominent market and garrison town, standing as it does guarding the 'Gap of the North' leading through the mountains to the south of the island.

In 1908, in his *Wanderings in Ireland*, M. M. Shoemaker remarked that 'This is the Protestant end of Ireland, prosperous and contented.' Indeed, the north-east of the island has always been the stronghold of Unionism. It was also the hotbed of the Industrial Revolution, in so far as it touched Ireland, fanning out from Belfast into the countryside of Down and Antrim.

With the emergence of the middle class, largely facilitated by this industrial boom, the notion of a seaside holiday became popular. Many coastal towns such as Bangor, Rostervor and Warrenpoint became favourite destinations from which to escape the daily grind of working life. These locations responded by providing entertainments and activities, such as baths and fairgrounds.

The coast was also a popular place of leisure for the better off, and many large villas were built to take advantage of the sea views and air. Of these, one of the grandest was Donard Lodge. This was a substantial granite mansion built by the 3rd Earl of Annesley. It was set within its own pleasure grounds on a hill, overlooking the sea, at Newcastle. It was demolished in 1966, but the view it was built to capture can still be appreciated by visitors today.

Opposite: Baths, Warrenpoint
Young boys enjoying their holiday dip at the seaside baths, Warrenpoint.

Of Industry and Leisure

Right: Linen Hall, Newry

The Linen Hall was built to the designs of the surveyor and architect Samuel Sproule in 1783. Its purpose was to enable the direct selling of linen from the surrounding area rather then via the Linen Hall in Dublin. It became a barracks in the 1870s and in 1923, when the army pulled out, a residential complex known as Linen Hall Square. That in turn was demolished to make way for the current Mourneview Park housing estate. The gateway seen here, ornamented with a carved harp and spinning wheel, survives, but the complex seen through the arch does not.

Below: Old Custom House, Merchant's Quay, Newry

Newry's Custom House dated to about 1750, closed in 1806 and became a prison, known as a bridewell, in 1820. It was a place of temporary confinement, holding prisoners until they could be moved to the county gaol. It was demolished in the 1960s.

Opposite: Switchback Railway, Bangor

Thompson's Gravity Patent Switchback, as this early roller-coaster was known, was the largest of its kind when erected in 1889. It would have been a huge attraction to the seaside holiday makers and day-trippers. It was sadly short-lived, being destroyed by 'the great gale' of 1894.

As Safe as Houses

Above and opposite: Mount Panther

Mount Panther began life as a large five-bay house of brick, built around 1740. It had a tripartite doorway with a Venetian window overhead and a semi-circular window above that again – typically Palladian. Between 1774 and 1760 it was home to the Very Rev. Patrick Delany and his wife, the well-known writer and artist, known to most today as Mrs Delany. In 1772 the house was bought by Francis Annesley, later 1st Earl of Annesley. He added three bay extensions to either end of the original house and covered the whole in stucco. His improvements also included redecoration of the main rooms with fine plasterwork in the style of the architect Robert Adam, the most impressive of which was the Ballroom.

During the Second World War the house was used as a furniture store and protected valuable pieces from Belfast City Hall from the blitz. In the 1960s, however, the burden of rates forced the removal of the roof and the stripping of most of the fittings. Since then the house has deteriorated badly and is today a ruined shell. Before it got quite so bad, mouldings were taken of some its plasterwork for the restoration of Malone House in Belfast.

Lakeside Retreat

Above and right: Great Northern Hotel, Rostrevor
Rostrevor was one of the finest hotels built by the enterprising railway companies of the nineteenth century. In this case an hotel, known as the Mourne Hotel, already existed when the Great Northern Railway took it over, extended it and opened it under their own name in the 1890s. Its grand design was redolent of a country house and its setting, on the shores of Carlingford Lough, little short of idyllic. Sadly it was one of the many architectural casualties of the Troubles in Northern Ireland, being fire-bombed in the 1980s.

Above: Market House, Knockchree Avenue, Kilkeel

This modest little Market House likely dated to the early 1800s. It provided a covered, arched ground floor that opened onto a small square, both of which would have provided space for the regular markets. The first floor housed the sittings of the court and provided space for social events such as music and dancing. It was demolished in 1956.

Above: Houses, Boat Street, Newry

This fantastic pair of houses likely dated to the late seventeenth or early eighteenth century. They were of a type known as 'Dutch Billys', a reference to their Dutch-style curved gables and King William of Orange who came from the Netherlands. They were usually built in pairs, sharing a large central chimneystack off which each would have been supported. The variety of different glazing suggests a long period of make-do and mend when each was probably occupied by several tenants at a time.

Early Influences

Opposite below: Canal Warehouses, Newry

These handsome houses above would have been built on the back of Newry's wealth, derived primarily from its trade in linen. As sad as their loss is, the loss of the warehouses that once supported them is also to be regretted.

Above and right: Gill Hall, Dromore

A large early house, Gill Hall dated to the 1670s and was built for one John Magill. Around 1736 it was enlarged, possibly to the designs of the well-known architect, Richard Castle, who may have been responsible for the bow-fronted wings seen at either end. It was decorated throughout with wooden panelling, and houses a grand staircase of barley-twist balusters. The house was reputedly one of the most haunted in Ireland, to the extent that the family vacated it in 1910 in favour of another property. During the Second World War it was occupied by the RAF, following which its condition deteriorated. While still in a salvageable condition, it was destroyed by fire in 1969.

Indian Summer

Above: Swimming Baths, Marine Road, Warrenpoint

This exotic structure evokes the Mughal palaces of India with its octagonal corner turrets and topee-like domes. It was built between 1906 and 1908 to the design of the firm Kaye-Perry & Ross. It would have been a popular destination, with open-air swimming pools, segregated for men and women, as well as baths of various temperatures within the building itself. It is today in a much-diminished state, its pools dry and all but its central 'tower' removed.

Opposite above: Cottage, Castlewellan

Castlewellan was home to the Annesley family, ennobled as Viscounts Glerawly and later as Earls Annesley. This 'cottage' was likely built about 1802 when the second Earl succeeded to the title. Its odd proportions, such as its low roof, suggest the renovation and extension of an earlier existing building rather than a completely new construction. Nonetheless it was an elegant villa and survived to about 1860. It was likely demolished when the family moved into the newly-completed Castlewellan Castle in 1859.

Opposite below: Donard Lodge, Newcastle

The Annesley family were also responsible for this handsome regency seaside villa, built for the 3rd Earl between 1829 and 1832. It was the result of two different designers – one, John Lynn, was responsible for the garden front and conservatory and the Belfast partnership of Duff and Jackson designed the entrance front. The main hall was entered through a door in the side of the central projection, under the colonnade. The house was requisitioned during the Second World War and later demolished, in 1966.

FERMANAGH

If Cavan is the lake district of Ireland then Fermanagh to its north can't fail to be its nearest challenger. The county is dominated by two vast expanses of water in the form of Upper and Lower Lough Earn. These drain the surrounding countryside of sloping valleys and rocky projections where pasture is the dominant form of agriculture.

The county, previously the stronghold of the Maguires, was included in the Plantation of Ulster following the capture of the strategic town of Enniskillen in 1607. It still remains the hub of the county with the main roads converging on it like the strings of a large web. It famously raised two regiments in the British Army, the Inniskilling Dragoons and the Royal Inniskilling Fusiliers, the names of both have since been lost through regimental amalgamation.

Belleek is the other well-known town of the county, famous today for the production of the pottery that bears its name. John Caldwell Bloomfield established the firm in 1857. Legend has it that his curiosity was ignited by the unusually fine and bright finish he noticed on his estate cottages and, making investigations, he discovered deposits of feldspar and kaolin on his land that could be used to make pottery. He harnessed the river to power a mill and began production of fine china that became famous for its creamy translucency and gentle sheen. Success was given a boost when Queen Victoria presented a Belleek China tea set to the German Royal Family, helping to spread its fame and popularity.

The county is also home to some of Ireland's finest houses, among them Florence Court and Castle Coole. Florence Court is a lucky survivor. It was transferred to the National Trust in 1953 and two years later a fire ripped through the upper floor of the house. Coupled with damage caused by the massive amounts of water pumped onto the flames, two thirds of the house was ruined. Clever thinking and prompt action led to holes being drilled in the dining room ceiling to allow the water pass through it without collapsing it. The house survives today, beautifully restored and run by the National Trust, as is Castle Coole, James Wyatt's *tour-de-force* of cool neoclassical rigour.

One house not so lucky was Castle Archdale. It replaced an earlier house destroyed during the Williamite wars and was commandeered during the Second World War. Its location on the shores of Lough Erne made it an ideal base for the flying boats of the No. 209 squadron of the RAF, and it was from here that they patrolled the north Atlantic. The house was kept on by the RAF until 1957 but, neglected, was demolished in 1970. Surviving today are the remains of three and a half sides of the courtyard, a large gap formed by the absence of the house, like a ring setting missing its diamond.

Opposite: East Bridge Street, Enniskillen
The street here is wide, clean and busy. Full of cars today, parked on either side and with a lane for driving in the middle, such streets appear much smaller than they do here.

Quiet Domesticity

Above and right: Belleek Hotel, Belleek

Like many early hotels, Belleek would have been modelled on a large private household and so it appeared as such from the outside, where it overlooked the River Erne. Within, the rooms would have been arranged similarly, with guests sometimes dining together in what would pass as the dining room of a fine private house of the time. The hotel still stands, though much altered and added to. The beautiful riverside gardens are no more and the building itself has been encased in later reworkings.

Above: RIC Barracks, Brookeborough

This is one of the few buildings illustrated that is wonderfully intact today. The Royal Irish Constabulary was established in 1822 and by 1900 there were around 1,600 barracks of various sizes spread across the island. They took a variety of styles, but many assumed the appearance of simple domestic dwellings. Huge amounts of them have not survived the turmoil of Irish history and this one, in Brookeborough, gives us some idea of what has been lost.

Right: Moat School, Lisnaskea

A typical school form, much like a church with its separate entrances for men and women, that would have been divided into two large rooms, one for girls and one for boys. This one had unusually fine-cut stone detailing around the windows and doors.

Lakeland Beauty

Left: Conservatory, Bellevue

It wasn't just the untamed wilds of nature that provided pleasure and leisure to those with the time and money to enjoy it, so too did the increasing popularity of horticulture. Here we see the grand glasshouse constructed at Bellevue in 1840 by Richard Turner who had designed the Palm Houses for the botanical gardens in Dublin and Belfast.

Opposite above: Steamer, Lough Erne

Below: General View, Enniskillen

The chief natural beauty of the county of Fermanagh is its lakes, Upper and Lower Lough Erne, both of which have been popular with visitors since tourism itself arrived in these parts. A popular way to see and explore the lakes was on a steamer, one of which can be seen filled with people (right). Notice that no one seems to be in the cabin below.

A similar steamer can be seen in the view of Enniskillen (below), which was the town picturesquely sandwiched between the upper and lower portions of Lough Erne.

Above: East Bridge Street, Enniskillen

This view, south-east, down East Bridge Street shows a prosperous later Victorian town. The grand building on the left was a branch of the Belfast Bank, constructed of red sandstone in 1880. It survives today as Danske Bank. Two doors up is a small two-storey house with a thatched roof, which does not. It was likely a survivor from the older town.

Left: Thatched Cottage, Letterbreen

A large, commodious house in the vernacular idiom, this was likely the home of a well-to-do farmer. Despite its traditional materials it has absorbed the architectural influences of the time and has large evenly spaced windows and two storeys. It represents a hybrid of sorts and the flexibility of the local self-builder.

Opposite: Castle Barracks, Enniskillen Castle, Enniskillen

Dating back to the 1400s, the castle was famously home to the Royal Inniskilling Fusiliers and the 5th Royal Inniskilling Dragoon Guards, which dated back to 1689. Here we can see their tents pitched in the yard. Today the Castle is home to both the Fermanagh County Museum and the Inniskillings Museum.

Above and right: Castle Hume, Derrygonnelly

Castle Hume marked an important milestone in Ireland in being the first commission of the architect Richard Castle. Built in 1728, almost immediately destroyed by fire and rebuilt by 1729, the house had been constructed for the MP Gustavus Hume. In the 1830s the main block was demolished to provide stone for a new house, Ely Lodge, on the same estate. It in turn was blown up as part of the 21st birthday celebrations of the 4th Marquess of Ely, who intended to build a new house, but this never came to fruition. All the Marquess was left with were the stables of the original house, shown here. Matching a small country house in their scale, within Castle created beautifully restrained, vaulted spaces for stalls. At the time, some horses would appear to have lived better than many of the local population.

Stately Piles

Above: Castle Archdale, Irvinestown

Castle Archdale was built about 1773 for Colonel Mervyn Archdale, replacing an earlier plantation castle of 1615. The house was six bays wide from the front, the central two bays breaking forward and bearing a tripartite entrance doorcase. The house sat in the middle of, and slightly forward of, one side of a courtyard, to which it was linked by small curved sweeps. It was occupied during the Second World War by the RAF, who continued in residence up until 1957. By that point the house had succumbed to the wear of its residents and was unroofed in 1957, eventually being demolished in 1970.

Classical Education

Above left: Inishmore Hall, Lisbelaw

This home of the Hall family, sometimes also known as Innismore, was constructed in the 1840s, possibly to the design of Richard Morrison. It was two storeys high and seven bays long, the central three bays being grouped behind a semi-circular entrance portico. It was demolished in the 1950s, but the portico was salvaged and reused at the Portora Royal School, Enniskillen.

Above right: Colebrooke School, Brookeborough

A rather grand schoolhouse, with classical portico, to which is attached a flagstaff. Behind its neat façade would likely have been two schoolrooms, one for girls and one for boys.

Opposite above: Castle Caldwell, Belleek

Castle Caldwell began life as a plantation castle in 1619. It was altered much over the centuries, notably in 1778 when large sums of money were spent on it. It was beset by fire in the early twentieth century and sold to the Forestry Commission in 1913. It is now an overgrown ruin.

Opposite below: Magheramena Castle, Belleek

This 'castle' was constructed to the designs of John B. Keane around 1840 for the Johnston family. It style was Elizabethan-revival, perhaps in an effort to reinforce the family's connections with and origins from that period. It was used as a parochial house before being unroofed and demolished in the 1950s. It is today an overgrown ruin.

MONAGHAN

Monaghan, given its diminutive size, might be thought an unlikely place to have looked for the heights of Victorian exuberance and fantasy, yet those who are familiar with the county and its history know different. The landscape is that of the Drumlin belt, with the odd lake here and there giving a clue to what watery scenery is to come further south and west. Nestled between the gentle valleys and glens of these geological bumps were, and to an extent still are, a treasure trove of architectural whimsy.

Of those in the following pages, several are probably quite well known to those who have delved into the pages of Monaghan's history. The most fantastical of them was undoubtedly Rossmore Castle, begun by the 2nd Lord Rossmore in 1827 and extended in 1858. Local story relates how the drawing room was extended several times in competition with the Shirleys of the Lough Fea estate, each vying to create the larger room. Despite its size, apparent from photographs, the Shirleys won. At its zenith the castle possessed three different towers and 117 windows, of 53 different shapes. To describe it as having been a complicated composition would be an understatement. Unfortunately, after the Second World War, dry rot was discovered to have penetrated much of the house and it was abandoned and finally demolished in 1974.

Another of these great Monaghan confections was Dartrey House, built in 1846 for the 3rd Lord Cremorne, subsuming and replacing an earlier Palladian house on the site. Dartrey was also born of the Victorian enthusiasm for all things medieval and Tudor. It had mullioned windows, curvilinear gables and what Mark Bence-Jones described as 'an army of Tudor chimneys'. The fortunes of the family declined however. In 1937 the contents of the house were sold and it was vacated due to its size and the cost of rates. The last owner, Lady Edith Anne Windham, daughter of the 2nd Earl of Dartrey, moved into the steward's house. A local story tells how she lent it for a charity ball to the RSPCA, after which the local council demanded a year's worth of rates be paid as the house, in their opinion, was still inhabited. Understandably annoyed by this cruel use of bureaucratic rules and book-following, she had the house demolished in 1946 so that no mistake could be made about whether she still resided there or not.

Opposite: The Old Infirmary, High Street, Monaghan
A stoic but handsome building, constructed in the late nineteenth century and incorporating remains of the earlier county gaol of 1821. It has been replaced by the current county hospital.

Victorian Fantasies

Above: Rossmore Castle, Monaghan

The vast, Gormenghastian complex of Rossmore was built around 1827 to 1830 to the designs of William Morrison, incorporating an earlier house on the site. It was enlarged upon in 1884 by William Deane Butler and again in 1888 by W. H. Lynn. The house survived the Troubles and the Second World War only to succumb to dry rot. It was abandoned in the 1940s and 30 years later what remained of it was blown up, in 1974, leaving little trace of it today.

Below: Castle Shane, Monaghan

The original castle on this site dated back as far as 1591. In 1836 the building was remodelled for the Lucas-Scudamore family in the Elizabethan or Jacobean style popular at the time. It was a handsome, busy house, animated with curved gables and chimneys. It was consumed by fire in 1920 and only some crumbling walls survive today.

Social Infrastructures

Opposite: St Macarthan's Cathedral, Monaghan

This soaring, fantastical cathedral was constructed between 1861, when the site was purchased, and 1892, when the building was dedicated and opened. It was designed by the architect J.J. McCarthy who died before it was completed, but whose design was faithfully carried out. The interior once matched the gothic magnificence of the exterior, with a grand baldacchino over the altar. Sadly, this was all stripped out around 1982 when efforts were made to bring the cathedral in line with Vatican II. It was the greatest loss that resulted from the reorganisation of Roman Catholic churches following the second Vatican Council.

Below left: Old Town Chapel, Park Street, Monaghan

This small chapel was constructed in 1824 and formed a beautiful, if discreet, addition to the street. It was a development on the traditional barn-like chapels of earlier times and prefaced Catholic Emancipation in 1829 by just a few years. Perhaps it was ornamented with its spikes and shamrock-like cross thereafter. It was demolished by William Hague to make way for the current church of St Joseph, constructed between 1897 and 1900.

Above: Train Station, Clones

Following the partition of Ireland in 1922 the two new states found themselves in possession of various branches of railway, which all together formed a network covering the island. Difficulties arose when one side decided to close their part of a particular track, and so it was with Clones. It closed in 1957 and here we see the station, from 1858, being dismantled.

Demolitions

Left: Newbliss House, Clones

Newbliss was the home of the Murray-Ker family, who had it constructed about 1814, replacing an earlier house of 1740. It was a relatively plain design, enlivened by the small porch in the Greek revival style that gave a focus to its entrance front. The house was demolished in the 1940s.

Above: Dartrey House, Rockcorry

Dartrey was a palatial Tudor-revival house built in 1846 to the design of William Burn. The Dawson family, for whom it was built, had come to Ireland from Yorkshire around 1600 and had been granted land in Monaghan following Cromwell's campaign in Ireland. The house that Burn built replaced an earlier one of 1750 known as Dawson's Grove and was a wondrous, picturesque confection. It stood, beautifully situated above Lough Dromore, until it was demolished in the 1940s to avoid rates.

Ebbing Hope

All: Hope Castle, Castleblayney

Hope Castle, or Blayney Castle, was designed by the architect Robert Woodgate in 1799 for the 11th Baron Blayney. It was a relatively small, five-bay house situated above the shore of Lough Muckno. It was bought by the Hope family, owners of the famous diamond, in 1853, and in the 1860s Henry Thomas Hope doubled the house in size with an extension (opposite above) and embellished it with curving parapets and other flourishes. One of its great spaces was the top-lit stair hall, in a stripped-back classical style (opposite below left), reminiscent of the work of the English architect John Soane, with whom Woodgate had studied. The rest of the house was similarly detailed (opposite below right). The estate also boasted a small temple, or summerhouse, from about 1850, overlooking the lake, which survives today as a ruin (above).

Hope Castle was rented by Queen Victoria's son the Duke of Connaught between 1900 and 1904, reputedly because of its closeness to Castle Leslie, and Leonie Leslie in particular. It was occupied during the Troubles of 1919–23 and served as a hospital and home to an order of Franciscan nuns before being bought by Monaghan County Council in the 1980s. They proceeded to demolish the additions made by Hope in the 1860s following which the house was set alight in 2010. What remains today, although not beyond saving, is a shadow of a once great house, but one dripping with curious social history.

TYRONE

Historically Tyrone was the heartland of the O'Neill clan, under whose reign it also included all of current Derry/Londonderry and portions of east Donegal. As part of the Tudor conquest of Ireland a system of surrender and regrant was implemented whereby the native Irish Chiefs would surrender their ancient titles and independence in return for a peerage in the English style, within the English system. Thus 'the O'Neill', as the chief or king was styled, became Earl of Tyrone in 1542.

The title devolved eventually on his grandson, the famous Hugh O'Neill, who took up arms against the Crown as in the nine years' war of 1594–1603. Although O'Neill, the Earl of Tyrone, and his allies were pardoned at the end of the war, the following peace was uneasy and riven with distrust. In 1607 an event known as the Flight of the Earls saw O'Neill and his allies depart Ireland for Europe in the hope of mustering support for another war against the English. They never returned.

The O'Neill lands were forfeited and a whole swathe of Ulster was opened up to plantation, the hope being to quell the local unrest with the importation of loyal subjects from England and Scotland. The plantation saw the creation of towns typical of its planned approach to settlement. They were laid out regimentally, generally several roads converging on a square or 'diamond' that was sometimes occupied by a church. These general principles were altered to suit local conditions, such as Moy (p. 393) where the diamond is converged upon by two roads, or Pomeroy (opposite), where there are three.

Strabane was an older settlement that had plantation planning-principles worked upon it. In 1752, a new market house was completed on the Main Street as a focus to the town's activities. It was a simple enough building with a tripartite, Venetian window over a large open arch in the gable end, which faced down the street. The side elevations had open arcades on the ground floor with regular rows of windows above them. In 1904 the Market House was expensively and controversially refurbished at which time a grand but awkward-looking clock tower was added to the south end. This hid what had been a restrained yet graceful elevation behind a slightly muddled construction, whose height and prominence were its only real saving graces.

From the early 1970s, with the outbreak of the troubles in Northern Ireland, Strabane suffered substantially from the violence. Shootings and bombings were commonplace. In February 1972 the Market House was damaged by a fire and later that year was finally destroyed by a 50lb bomb. As well as taking with it the original building and its ungainly extension, the bomb also destroyed a large amount of local historical records. Today the site is partially occupied by a car park.

Opposite: Town of Pomeroy, from the air
The town of Pomeroy is a classic example of the kind of town laid out during the plantation period, with straight streets, organised geometrically and converging on a square, frequently known as a diamond.

Towering Presence

Left: Drum Manor, Kildress

A Tudor-revival house of 1829 designed by Major Richardson Brady, it was a pleasing if somewhat typical house of its type. It was given an architectural jolt with additions made by the architect William Hastings, including the four-storey tower that can be seen here. The house was largely demolished in 1975, though the tower was left. It is today a picturesque ruin.

Right: Town Hall, Strabane

The tower of Strabane Town Hall is an ungainly composition, consisting of five parts, each a little different from the other in style so that, when composed one on top of the other they create an awkward and disjointed structure. The tower was added in 1904 to the existing market hall of 1752, which can be seen poking out on either side of it. It was destroyed by an IRA bomb in 1972.

Below: Abercorn Square, Strabane

A respectable and elegant shop front with ionic columns supporting an entablature, decorated with the painted name of the shop. It's an unusually urbane and grand design, dating to the early part of the nineteenth century. It no longer survives.

Curious Mixes

Left: Richmond Lodge, Ballygawley
This former rectory was built about 1870. It is a pleasing, simple house of good proportions. It still survives today, with slight alterations.

Below: Gate Lodge, Corcreevy House, Fivemiletown
This gate lodge, probably dating from the latter part of the nineteenth or early part of the twentieth century, is a curious case. Modelled in the style of a vernacular house or 'Irish Cottage' it illustrated a developing appreciation by the upper classes of the native traditions and culture.

Above: Northland House, Dungannon

Northland House was home of the Knox family, later Earls of Ranfurly, and at different times throughout its history was known as Northland Park and as Dungannon Park. It began life around 1785, and was added to by the architect Robert Woodgate about 1799. It underwent further work in 1840 and again in 1846, all of which resulted in a large, classical and vaguely institutional-looking mass of building. Following the First World War and the decline of the family's fortunes the contents were sold in 1927 and the house shortly afterward. It was demolished in the 1930s.

Right: Cecil Manor, Augher

Cecil Manor was a rather stern and stark house built around 1829 to the designs of the architect William Farrell. While quite austere its proportions and composition were pleasing in their own way. The manor was home to the Gervais family who were of French Huguenot descent. No trace of it survives today.

Urban Elegance

Left: Gortmerron House, Anne Street, Dungannon

A beautiful and accomplished five-bay, three-storey house built about 1780 for one John Wilcocks, a local man involved in the linen trade. It later became home to the Technical Institute, the lettering of which can be seen clinging on to the façade. It was derelict by the 1970s and no longer survives.

Below: George's Street, Dungannon

This image shows George's Street on a market day, looking north-west, with carts lined up on either side of the street. The view is closed by the small Court House of 1830. Very little, if anything, survives of this view. The courthouse has been altered and is now in a state of decline while most of the buildings on either side, including the Northland Arms Hotel, have since been replaced by modern structures.

Above: Moy, from the air

The town of Moy was laid out in the 1760s by the 1st Earl of Charlemont. It was reputedly modelled on the town of Bosco Marengo in Piedmont, Italy, which the earl had seen on his travels, yet it could also said to be derived from the plantation towns of the 1600s. Perhaps it is a hybrid of both. Its large, long central square is today somewhat over-used as a carpark.

Rambling Mansions

Above: Aughentaine Castle, Fivemiletown

A lightly Italianate house of two storeys built to the designs of the architect T.R. Browne in 1860. It had the peculiar addition of two campanile-like towers at either end that lent it an almost symmetrical and vaguely institutional appearance. It was sold in 1954 and demolished shortly after by its new owner, who replaced it with a modern house in the classical idiom.

Opposite: Roxborough Castle, Moy

Roxborough was a bulky, looming mansion that was home to the Earls of Charlemont. The original house was constructed in 1738 and was enlarged twice. In 1842 it was given two wings by the architect William Murray and in 1864 these were enlarged by William J. Barre so that they framed the original house. The result transformed a simple five-bay, three-storey Georgian house into a French-style chateau with high mansard roofs. The house was burnt out in 1922.

INDEX

ACKNOWLEDGEMENTS

This is my first effort at putting together a book of my own and as such there are many people who deserve my gratitude and thanks.

Firstly I would like to thank Jarlath Gregory and Brian Nicholson, each of whom, at the beginning of this project, gave freely of their time, experience, expertise and friendship in an effort to set me off in the right direction.

This book would not have been possible without the photographs it showcases; indeed, they are really what it is all about. A variety of institutions, and their staff, were kind enough to allow me access to their collections, and to give permission to publish images in their care. They include Colum O'Riordan, Eve McAulay, Simon Lincoln, Anne Henderson, Aisling Dunne and David Griffin at the Irish Architectural Archive; Glenn Dunne, Keith Murphy, Berni Metcalfe and Máire Ní Chonalláin at the National Library of Ireland; Aaron Binchy at the Royal Society of Antiquaries of Ireland; Críostóir Mac Cárthaigh at the National Folklore Collection; Patria McWalter at the Galway County Council Archives; Grace Moloney, Deborah Flack and Father John Chester at Clogher Historical Society; Michael Byrne at the Offaly History Centre; Tony Roche at the National Monuments Service; Brett Irwin and Craig Murray at the Public Record Office of Northern Ireland; Philippa Martin at the Ulster Architectural History Society; Louise Cooling and Jackson Pearce at the Victoria and Albert Museum; Justin Hobbs at Time Inc; Roy Byrne at Christ Church Cathedral; Finbar Connolly at the National Museum of Ireland; Terence Reeves-Smith at the Historic Environment Division of the Department of the Environment, Northern Ireland; and individually Sean Gill, J.A.K. Deane, George Gossip and David Bland.

It has not been possible to visit the site of every building featured within and so I accept there may be mistakes. For proof-reading parts of the text and pointing out inaccuracies I am truly grateful to Matthew Maxwell and Michael Seery, each of whom were kind enough to look over different parts of this project at various times. Whatever inaccuracies remain are entirely my own responsibility.

For the work of marshalling text and images on the page and for transforming them from individual fragments into a cohesive whole, my deep gratitude is due to Vicky Barnard, Andy Chapman and Hannah Porter of Plum5, whose patience, guidance and expertise have transformed this book into the beautiful object you hold in your hands today. Credit is also due to Rebecca Lee and Henrietta Drane for their editorial expertise.

I would also like to thank my colleagues at Dublin Castle, in particular Mary Heffernan, Jenny Papassotiriou and Cormac Molloy who were kind enough, as I reached the final stages of this project, to accommodate my requests for time off.

Finally, but by no means least, I would like to thank my work colleagues, my friends and my family. Over the last 10 months or so that have I have spent gathering photographs, researching and writing, they have been kind enough to understand my workload and not question why I might be so reclusive, while being there to lend their support, encouragement and good humour when most needed. To my parents in particular I offer my deepest thanks.

Will Derham, 2015

DEDICATION

For Phil – I hope you'd have been impressed.

SOURCES

Online

Archiseek www.archiseek.com

David Hicks www.davidhicksbook.blogspot.ie

Dictionary of Irish Architects www.dia.ie

The Irish Aesthete www.theirishaesthete.com

Landed Estates Database www.landedestates.ie

Lord Belmont in Northern Ireland
www.lordbelmontinnorthernireland.blogspot.ie

National Inventory of Architectural Heritage
www.buildingsofireland.ie

Turtle Bunbury www.turtlebunbury.com

Books

A Field Guide to the Buildings of Ireland
Sean Rothery (Dublin, 1997).

The Buildings of Ireland: North Leinster
Christine Casey & Alistair Rowan (London, 1993).

The Buildings of Ireland: North West Ulster
Alistair Rowan (London, 1979).

The Buildings of Ireland: South Ulster
Kevin V. Mulligan (London, 2013).

Burke's Guide to Country Houses, Volume 1: Ireland
Mark Bence-Jones (London, 1980).

Classic Irish Houses of the Middle Size
Maurice Craig (Dublin, 2006).

The Decline of the Big House in Ireland
Terence Dooley, (Dublin, 2001).

Dublin 1660 – 1860: The Shaping of a City
Maurice Craig (Dublin, 2006).

The Heart of Dublin
Peter Pearson (Dublin, 2000).

The Houses of Ireland
Brian de Breffny & Rosemary ffolliott (London, 1992).

Ireland's Civil Engineering Heritage
Ronald Cox & Philip Donald (Cork, 2013).

Ireland's vernacular Heritage
Kevin Danaher (Cork, 1975).

The Irish Country House: It's Past, Present and Future
Terence Dooley & Christopher Ridgway (Dublin, 2015).

The Irish Georgian Society: A Celebration
Robert O'Byrne (Dublin, 2008).

The Scenery and Antiquities of Ireland
J. Stirling Coyne (London, 2003).

A Lost Tradition
Niall McCullough & Valerie Mulvin (Dublin, 1987).

Tourist's Gaze: Travellers to Ireland, 1800-2000
Glenn Hooper (Cork, 2001).

Twilight of the Ascendency
Mark Bence-Jones (London, 1987)

Vanishing Country Houses of Ireland
The Knight of Glin, David J. Griffin & Nicholas K Robinson (Dublin, 1989).

The Victorian Visitor in Ireland
Donal Horgan (Cork, 2002).

The Blitz: Belfast in the War years
by Brain Barton (Belfast, 1989).

Bombs on Belfast: the Blitz, 1941
by Ian Adamson & Christopher D. McGimpsey (Belfast, 2011).

PICTURE CREDITS